Copyright © 2014 by: Tuchy Palmieri
All rights reserved.

ISBN: 1-4943-0161-X
ISBN-13: 9781494301613

Emmet Fox was not directly associated with the recovery movements of his time. He is however noted for his contributions to people in recovery. Many of his booklets found themselves in the hands of people working the 12 step programs. We have reprinted several Of his booklets and created a book form his pamphlet's that have helped thousands of People in all walks of life to find comfort, peace of mind, and serenity. May this book help keep the miracle of recovery alive today.

In Gratitude

Tuchy Palmieri
Healing Habits

Table of Contents

The Golden Key	1
Getting results by prayer	7
You Must Be Born Again	15
The Great Adventure	21
The Seven Day Mental Diet	29
Be Still	49
The Wonder Child	67
The Lion's Den	85
Faith	97
The Zodiac And The Bible	103
The Secret Place	129
Light And Salvation	157
No Results Without Prayer	171
The Garden Of Allah	175

FOREWORD

I have compressed this booklet into six pages. Had it been possible I would have reduced it to six lines. It is not intended to be an instructional treatise, but a practical recipe for getting out of trouble. Study and research are well in their own time and place, but no amount of either will get you out of a concrete difficulty. Nothing but <u>practical work in your own consciousness</u> will do that. The mistake made by many people, when things go wrong, is to skim through book after book, without getting anywhere.

Read the Golden Key several times. DO exactly what it says, and if you are persistent enough you will overcome any difficulty.

Emmet Fox

THE GOLDEN KEY

Scientific prayer will enable you, sooner or later, to get yourself, or anyone else, out of any difficulty on the face of the earth. It is the Golden Key to harmony and happiness.

To those who have no acquaintance with the mightiest power in existence, this may appear to be a rash claim, but it needs only a fair trial to prove that, without a shadow of doubt, it is a just one. You need take no one's word for it, and you should not. Simply try it for yourself, and see.

God is omnipotent, and man is His image and likeness, and has dominion over all things. This is the inspired teaching, and it is intended to be taken literally, at its face value. Man means every man, and so the ability to draw on this power is not the special prerogative of the Mystic or the Saint, as is so often supposed, or even of the highly-trained practitioner. Whoever you are, wherever you may be, the Golden Key to harmony is in your hand now. This is because in scientific prayer it is God who works, and not you, and so your particular limitations or weaknesses are of no account in the process. You are only the channel through which the Divine action takes place, and your treatment will really be just the getting of yourself out of the way. Beginners often get startling results at the first time of trying, for all that is absolutely essential is to have an open mind, and sufficient faith to try the experiment. Apart from that, you may hold any views on religion, or none.

As for the actual method of working, like all fundamental things, it is simplicity itself. All that you have to do is this: *Stop thinking about the difficulty, whatever it is, and think about God instead.* This is the complete rule, and if only you will do this, the trouble, whatever it is, will presently disappear. It makes no difference what kind of trouble it is. It may be a big thing or a little thing; it may concern health, finance, a law-suit, a quarrel, an accident, or anything else conceivable; but whatever it is, just stop thinking about it, and think of God instead— that is all you have to do.

The thing could not be simpler, could it? God Himself could scarcely have made it simpler, and yet it never fails to work when given a fair trial.

Do not try to form a picture of God, which is, of course, impossible. Work by rehearsing anything or everything that you know about God. God is Wisdom, Truth, inconceivable Love. God is present everywhere; has infinite power; knows everything; and so on. It matters not how well you may think you understand these things; go over them repeatedly.

But you must stop thinking of the trouble, whatever it is. The rule is to think about God, and if you are thinking about your difficulty you are not thinking about

God. To be continually glancing over your shoulder, as it were, in order to see how matters are progressing, is fatal, because that is thinking of the trouble, and you must think of God, and of nothing else. Your object is to drive the thought of the difficulty right out of your consciousness, for a few moments at least, substituting for it the thought of God. This is the crux of the whole thing. If you can become so absorbed in this consideration of the spiritual world that you really forget for a while all about the trouble concerning which you began to pray, you will presently find that you are safely and comfortably out of your difficulty—that your demonstration is made.

In order to "Golden Key" a troublesome person or a difficult situation, think, "Now I am going to 'Golden Key' John, or Mary, or that threatened danger"; then proceed to drive all thought of John, or Mary, or the danger right out of your mind, replacing it by the thought of God.

By working in this way about a person, you are not seeking to influence his conduct in any way, except that you prevent him from injuring or annoying you, and you do him nothing but good. Thereafter he is certain to be in some degree a better, wiser, and more spiritual person, just because you have "Golden Keyed" him. A pending lawsuit or other difficulty would probably fade out harmlessly without coming to a crisis, justice being done to all parties concerned.

If you find that you can do this very quickly, you may repeat the operation several times a day with intervals between. Be sure, however, each time you have done it, that you drop all thought of the matter until the next time. This is important.

We have said that the Golden Key is simple, and so it is, but, of course, it is not always easy to turn. If you are very frightened or worried it may be difficult, at first, to get your thoughts away from material things. But by constantly repeating some statement of absolute Truth that appeals to you, such as *There is no power but God*, or *I am the child of God, filled and surrounded by the perfect peace of God*, or *God is Love*, or *God is guiding me now*, or, perhaps best and simplest of all, just *God is with me*—however mechanical or dead it may seem at first—you will soon find that the treatment has begun to "take," and that your mind is clearing. Do not struggle violently; be quiet but insistent. Each time that you find your attention wandering, just switch it straight back to God.

Do not try to think out in advance what the solution of your difficulty will probably turn out to be. This is technically called "outlining," and will only delay the demonstration. Leave the question of ways and means strictly to God. You want to get out of your difficulty—that is sufficient. You do your half, and God will never fail to do His.

Whosoever shall call upon the name of the Lord shall be saved.

Getting Results by Prayer

A GREAT deal of confusion seems to exist in many minds concerning the precise avenue through which the Divine Power is to be approached, and realization and harmony attained. So many schools of thought seem to be competing for the attention of the student; so busy is the printing press; so many new books and pamphlets are written; so many magazines come and go; that people have told me that they have felt quite in despair of ever discovering what it really is that they must do to be saved.

Sometimes it seems as though the story of Babel were repeating itself in the metaphysical movement—and yet we all know in our hearts that the true Gate is narrow and the real Way strait. One well known Eastern teacher of great spiritual power has actually published a pamphlet from which it appears that the genuine criterion of authenticity is to have no Path at all. This is the *reductio ad absurdum* which pulls us up short and restores the light.

The truth, of course, is this, that the only solution of the problem is definitely to contact the Divine Power which dwells within your own soul; and, having consciously done that, to bring it to bear upon the various difficulties in your life, taking them in due order, that is, attacking the most urgent first. This is the right way of working, and it is the only way that can possibly help you, or your affairs, in the long run. The real remedy for every one of your difficulties is, as we are told on every page of the Bible, to find and *know* the Indwelling Presence. *Acquaint now thyself with Him and be at peace. In His Presence is fulness of joy. Behold, I am with you alway.*

This, then, is the task, and the only one—to find, and consciously know, your own Indwelling Lord.

You see now how the confusion disappears, melts away, and the perfect simplicity of the whole thing emerges once you realize this fact. From this it necessarily follows that all schools and churches; all teachers, under whatever name they may be called; all the textbooks, magazines, pamphlets, and what-not; are but temporary expedients for enabling you to make this contact. In themselves they are of no importance except as a means to an end. The best mode of approach to Divine things for you is the one that happens to make it easiest for you to locate the Inner Light within yourself.

Such things as temperament, education, family tradition, and so on, will make one book, or one teacher, or one school, more useful than another; but never as anything more than the means to a certain end. That end is effective self discovery. "Man know *thyself*"—thy true self which is the Divine I Am. And so we see that the best "movement," the finest textbook, the greatest teacher, is just the one that happens best to fit the individual need. It is entirely a practical matter, and the only test that ever could, or ever will, be of any use, is the practical one of *judgment by results*. Of course, Jesus anticipated this difficulty, and met it, as he has met all our difficulties. He gave us the simple and perfect standard: *By their fruits ye shall know them.*

The great peril to true religion has always been the building up of vested interests in wealthy organizations, or in the exploitation by individuals of their own personalities. An organized church is always in danger of developing into an "industry" which has to provide a living for numerous officials. When this happens the rank and file are sure to be severely discouraged from seeking spiritual things for themselves at first hand. A tradition of "loyalty" to the organization is built up as a means of self protection. Not loyalty to Truth, or to your own soul, be it remarked, but to the ecclesiastical machine. Thus the means becomes an end in itself and spiritual power then fades out. Rash promises and vague claims take the place of real verifiable demonstrations.

In the case of leaders who exploit their own personalities, the student is discouraged from going elsewhere for enlightenment or help; and here again "loyalty" to something other than God is allowed to block the avenue of Truth, and therefore becomes antichrist. What is this but the jealousy of the petty tradesman who warns a doubtful customer of the danger he runs in going to the "shop next door."

Remember that you absolutely owe no loyalty whatever to anything or anyone but your own soul and to the furtherance of its spiritual development. Your most solemn duty is to make everything secondary to that. "To thine own self be true; and it must follow, as the night the day, thou canst not then be false to any man."—*Shakespeare.*

The first step that the earnest student must take is to settle on a definite method of working, selecting whichever one seems to suit him best, and then giving it a fair trial. That means that you must acquire a definite method or system of spiritual treatment or scientific prayer. Merely reading books, making good resolutions, or talking plausibly about the thing will get you nowhere. *Get a definite method of working,* practise it conscientiously every day; and stick to one method long enough to give it a fair chance. You would not expect to play the violin after two or three attempts, or to drive a car without a little preliminary practice.

Having got your method, set to work definitely on some concrete problem in your own life, choosing preferably whichever is causing you the most trouble at the moment, or, better still, *whatever it is that you are most afraid of.* Work at it steadily; and if nothing has happened, if no improvement at all shows itself within, say, a couple of weeks at the outside, then try it on another problem. If you still get no result, then scrap that method and adopt a new one. Remember, *there is a way out;* that is as certain as the rising of the sun. The problem really is, not the getting rid of your difficulties, but the finding of your own best method for doing it.

If ill health is your difficulty, do not rest until you have brought about at least one bodily healing. There is no malady that has not been healed by someone at some time, and what others have done you can do, for God is Principle, and Principle changes not.

If poverty is the trouble, go to work on that, and clear it up once and for all. It can be done. It has been done. Others have done it, and you can.

If you are unhappy, dissatisfied with your lot, or your surroundings, above all, with yourself, set to work on that; refuse to take no for an answer; and insist upon the happiness and satisfaction that are yours by Divine right.

If your need is self-expression—artistic, literary, or otherwise—if your heart's desire is to attain to eminence in a profession, or some kind of public career, that, too, approached in the right spirit, is a legitimate and worthy object, and the right method of scientific prayer will bring you the prize.

Keep a record of your results, and on no account be satisfied with anything less than success. Above all things, avoid the deadly error of making excuses. There are no excuses for failing to demonstrate. When you do not demonstrate, it never by any chance means anything except that you have not worked in the right way. Excuses are the true and veritable devil, who comes to tempt you to remain outside the Kingdom of Heaven, while the Gate stands open. Excuses, in fact, are the only enemy that you really need to fear.

Find the method that suits you; cultivate simplicity—simplicity and spontaneity are the secret of effective prayer—work away steadily; *keep your own counsel; and whatsoever ye shall ask in My name, that will I do.*

You Must Be Born Again

WE are told concerning the teaching of Jesus that the common people heard him gladly. This could easily have been inferred from the most superficial study of the Gospels. The "man in the street," unsophisticated by theology or philosophy, has an intuitive perception of fundamental Truth when he meets it, that is often lacking in highly trained minds. Intellectual attainments may easily beget spiritual pride, and this is the only sin upon which Our Lord was severe. Yet among the learned, too, there were those, the more spiritually minded, who felt themselves attracted to the new Teacher. He was unconventional, hopelessly out of favor with the ecclesiastical authorities, a flouter of hallowed traditions; and yet, deep calleth unto deep, and so he had his friends and followers in high places also. One of these who felt irresistibly drawn to seek for further light was Nicodemus. He had the thirst for Divine things that will not be denied, but moral courage was not his strong point, and so he sought out the Teacher by night. That he should have gone at all was proof of the compelling power of the urge. Clearly the unfoldment of his spiritual nature was, in spite of defects in character, the principal thing in his life, and clearly he was dissatisfied with the progress he was making. Jesus, he believed, had something to give that was vital, and that gift might be just the secret that had hitherto eluded him, just the key he needed to unlock the spiritual treasure-house of his soul. Jesus might be able to show him why he had so far failed to attain; why, as we should say in modern phraseology, he had failed to demonstrate. And the Master's explanation was simple, concise, almost overwhelming in its directness. He said: *"You must be born again."*

This statement sums up the whole science of demonstration as it is practised on the spiritual basis. It is verily a textbook on metaphysics compressed into five words. It tells the whole story. You stand where you do today, wherever that is, because you are the man that you are. There is only one way under heaven by which you can be brought to stand anywhere else, and that is by becoming another man. The man you are cannot stand anywhere else; a different man cannot stand where you are now. If you wish to go up higher you can do so, and there is no limit to the height which you can attain upon that flight; but *you must be born again!*

Why is it that we make so little progress, compared, that is to say, with what we might and should make in view of the knowledge that we all, in this movement, possess—at least in theory? Why do we not change day by day and week by week from glory to glory, until our friends can scarcely recognize us for the same man or woman? Why should we not march about the world looking like gods, and feeling it; healing instantaneously all who come to us; reforming the sinner; setting the captives free; and generally "doing the works"? "Who did hinder you?"

And the reply is that demonstration, like all other things, has its price; that the price is that we be *born again,* and that in our secret hearts, too often, that is a price that we are not prepared to pay. We are in love with the present man, and all the things that constitute him, and we are not prepared to slay him that the other may be born.

We come into Truth with our little finger, and the great things will not come to us until we come in with the entire body; and there's the rub.

To come into Truth with your whole body is to bring every conscious thought and belief to the touchstone of Divine Intelligence and Divine Love. It is to reject every single thing, mental or physical, that does not square with that standard. It is to revise every opinion, every habit of thought, every policy, every branch of practical conduct, without any exception whatever.

YOU MUST BE BORN AGAIN

This, of course, is something absolutely tremendous. It is no mere spring cleaning of the soul. It is nothing less than a wholesale tearing down and rebuilding of the entire house. Is it any wonder that all but the very strongest spirits shirk it. And yet, is it any wonder that without it one never really does get anywhere.

It means, as St. Paul said, "dying daily." It means parting with all the prejudices that you have inherited and acquired during all your life long. It means taking the knife to all the little faults of character, petty vanities, minor deceits, and all those lesser forms of selfishness and pride that crystallize your spiritual joints, and are so dear to you. It may mean giving up the biggest thing in your present life, but if it does—well, that is the price that must be paid, and that is all about it.

If you are not prepared to pay this price, well and good; but you must not expect to receive from the Law more than you pay for. A little finger in Truth is well, but it can only produce a little finger result. For a full-length demonstration the whole body must be full of light. *You must be born again.*

The Great Adventure

MANY people seem to have the impression that the sole object of Divine Science is the overcoming of difficulties; but to suppose that, is to lose all sense of proportion. The Truth is to be sought for its own sake. The knowledge of Truth is its own reward, and that reward is health, harmony, and prosperity, to begin with; but this is only the beginning. The real object of the seeker should be the development of his own higher faculties and powers; in a word, his Spiritual Evolution.

Now it so happens that as fast as one acquires spiritual understanding, his circumstances improve in every respect—his health, his temper, his happiness and his material surroundings rapidly and automatically change for the better. *Per contra*, a want of true understanding automatically and necessarily expresses itself in some sort of difficulty on the physical plane, culminating in sin, sickness, and death.

When people find themselves in any difficulty, should they have some glimmerings of spiritual truth, they realize, however dimly, that a way out is to be found along the path of spiritual enlightenment, and consequently they study books, consult friends in the movement, ask for treatment or guidance, or take whatever step appears to be appropriate at the moment. This is the natural and proper course to pursue, and, provided they understand what it is that they are doing, it is only a matter of time before their difficulties—their ill-health, their poverty, their trouble, whatever it is—must disappear. They are, in fact, seeking spiritual enlightenment; they are working for a change in consciousness; and one cannot seek for an improved consciousness without getting it, nor get it without making a demonstration. To know this is to have "come into Truth," to use the common phrase.

Misunderstanding and disappointment

arise when people mistake the teaching for some kind of elaborate conjuring trick. When a man supposes that by a wave of the hand, or the repetition of an incantation, his circumstances can be changed for the better without any corresponding change in his own mentality, he is doomed to disappointment. He has not come into Truth, and the Truth movement has nothing for him.

During the past few years a large number of people of all sorts have consulted me about their difficulties, and they easily divide themselves into those two groups. Some people, for instance, are in trouble owing to some very obvious defect in character, but are quite unwilling to overcome this defect, or even, in many cases, to acknowledge it; they wish to continue in their mistake and to have prosperity or happiness as well. Needless to say, for them there is no relief until they have suffered a little more, and have been punished sufficiently to make them do what is necessary. The man who drinks, for example, is certain to ruin his business, and you cannot help him as long as he prefers whiskey to prosperity. Of course, if he is trying to give up whiskey, you can help him to do so, and then all will be well, but otherwise he will just have to go on suffering until his lesson is learned. Other people complain that they have no friends, cannot keep servants, and that they live unhappy, isolated lives; and a few minutes' conversation makes it obvious that there is an atrociously bad temper there which has driven everyone away. If such people are prepared to work to change themselves, the road is clear; but until they are, there is very little to be done for them.

Most of you who read this, however, will be seeking the Truth in the right way, and to seek the Truth in that spirit is really to have come into Truth. "You would not have sought Me had you not already found Me." That being so, you should not allow yourself to be worried or depressed merely because the demonstration is delayed. If you have sufficient understanding to believe in treatment, you have sufficient understanding to know that it must be only a matter of time before you are out of the wood—and what does it really matter whether it is a little sooner or a little later. Any delay in getting results can only be due to one of two things: Either the mental cause of your difficulty is very deeply seated in your consciousness and is requiring a good deal of work; or else you are not yet working in the best way, and if this is so, again it will be only a matter of time before you find what is the best way for you. In other words, once you are on the Path there is no hurry. "Oh, but," says someone, "in my case there is the most urgent hurry, because unless I make my demonstration by Saturday the verdict of the Court will be given against me," or "my creditors will foreclose," or "I shall lose the boat," or what not. But the answer in Truth is still—*There is no hurry,* for the gates of hell shall never prevail. Let evil do its worst on Saturday; let the Court give its verdict; let the creditors strike their blow;

let the boat sail. When Monday comes, prayer will still put everything right, if you can get your realization, and if not on Monday, then Wednesday, or Friday, or the week after next. Time does not really matter, for prayer is creative, and will build the New Jerusalem for you anywhere, at any time, irrespective of what may have happened, just as soon as you can get your realization of Truth, Omnipresent Good—Emanuel, which is God with you. This is the New Jerusalem which comes down out of heaven like a bride adorned for her husband, and is independent of any conditions on the physical plane.

When you are in difficulties, look upon the overcoming of them as a great adventure. Resist the temptation to be tragic, to give way to self-pity or discouragement; and approach the problems as though you were an explorer seeking a path through Darkest Africa, or an Edison working to overcome difficulties in connection with a new invention. You know that there is a way out of any difficulty whatever, no matter what it may be, through the changing of your own consciousness by prayer. You know that by thus raising your consciousness any conceivable form of good that you can desire will be yours; and you know that nobody else can by any means hinder you from doing this when you really want to do it—relatives, customers, employers, the government, bad times, so-called—nothing can hinder you from the rebuilding of your own consciousness—and this rebuilding is the Great Adventure.

The Seven Day Mental Diet

THE subject of diet is one of the foremost topics of the present day in public interest. Newspapers and magazines teem with articles on the subject. The counters of the bookshops are filled with volumes unfolding the mysteries of proteins, starches, vitamins, and so forth. Just now the whole world is food-conscious. Experts on the subject are saying that physically you become the thing that you eat— that your whole body is really composed of the food that you have eaten in the past. What you eat today, they say, will be in your bloodstream after the lapse of so many hours, and it is your blood-stream that builds all the tissues composing your body -and there you are.

Of course, no sensible person has any quarrel with all this. It is perfectly true, as far as it goes, and the only surprising thing is that it has taken the world so long to find it out; but in this pamphlet I am going to deal with the subject of dieting at a level that is infinitely more profound and far-reaching in its effects. I refer of course to *mental* dieting.

The most important of all factors in your life is the mental diet on which you live. It is the food which you furnish to your mind that determines the whole character of your life. It is the thoughts you allow yourself to think, the subjects that you allow your mind to dwell upon, which make you and your surroundings what they are. *As thy days, so shall thy strength be.* Everything in your life today—the state of your body, whether healthy or sick, the state of your fortune, whether prosperous or impoverished, the state of your home, whether happy or the reverse, the present condition of every phase of your life in fact—is entirely conditioned by the thoughts and feelings which you have entertained in the past, by the habitual tone of your past thinking. And the condition of your life tomorrow, and next week, and next year, will be entirely conditioned by the thoughts and feelings which you choose to entertain from now onwards.

In other words, you choose your life, that is to say, you choose all the conditions of your life, when you choose the thoughts upon which you allow your mind to dwell. Thought is the real causative force in life, and there is no other. You cannot have one kind of mind and another kind of environment. This means that you cannot change your environment while leaving your mind unchanged, nor—and this is the supreme key to life and the reason for this pamphlet —can you change your mind without your environment changing too.

This then is the real key to life: if you change your mind your conditions must change too—your body must change, your daily work or other activities must change; your home must change; the color-tone of your whole life must change—for whether you be habitually happy and cheerful, or low-spirited and fearful, depends entirely on the quality of the mental food upon which you diet yourself.

Please be very clear about this. If you change your mind your conditions must change too. *We are transformed by the renewing of our minds.* So now you will see that your mental diet is really the most important thing in your whole life.

This may be called the Great Cosmic Law, and its truth is seen to be perfectly obvious when once it is clearly stated in this way. In fact, I do not know of any thoughtful person who denies its essential truth. The practical difficulty in applying it, however, arises from the fact that our thoughts are so close to us that it is difficult, without a little practice, to stand back as it were and look at them objectively.

Yet that is just what you must learn to do.

You must train yourself to choose the subject of your thinking at any given time, and also to choose the emotional tone, or what we call the mood that colors it. Yes, you can choose your moods. Indeed, if you could not you would have no real control over your life at all. Moods habitually entertained produce the characteristic disposition of the person concerned, and it is his disposition that finally makes or mars a person's happiness.

You cannot be healthy; you cannot be happy; you cannot be prosperous; if you have a bad disposition. If you are sulky, or surly, or cynical, or depressed, or superior, or frightened half out of your wits, your life cannot possibly be worth living. Unless you are determined to cultivate a good disposition, you may as well give up all hope of getting anything worth while out of life, and it is kinder to tell you very plainly that this is the case.

If you are not determined to start in now and carefully select all day the kind of thoughts that you are going to think, you may as well give up all hope of shaping your life into the kind of thing that you want it to be, because this is the only way.

In short, if you want to make your life happy and worth while, which is what God wishes you to make it, you must begin immediately to train yourself in the habit of thought selection and thought control. This will be exceedingly difficult for the first few days, but if you persevere you will find that it will become rapidly easier, and it is actually the most interesting experiment that you could possibly make. In fact, this thought control is the most thrillingly interesting hobby that anyone could take up. You will be amazed at the interesting things that you will learn about yourself, and you will get results almost from the beginning.

Now many people knowing this truth, make sporadic efforts from time to time to control their thoughts, but the thought stream being so close, as I have pointed out, and the impacts from outside so constant and varied, they do not make very much progress. That is not the way to work. Your only chance is definitely to form a new habit of thought which will carry you through when you are preoccupied or off your guard as well as when you are consciously attending to the business. This new thought habit must be definitely acquired, and the foundation of it can be laid within a few days, and the way to do it is this:

Make up your mind to devote one week solely to the task of building a new habit of thought, and during that week let everything in life be unimportant as compared with that. If you will do so, then that week will be the most significant week in your whole life. It will literally be the turning-point for you. If you will do so, it is safe to say that your whole life will change for the better. In fact, nothing can possibly remain the same. This does not simply mean that you will be able to face your present difficulties in a better spirit; it means that the difficulties will go. This is the scientific way to Alter Your Life, and being in accordance with the Great Law it cannot fail. Now do you realize that by working in this way you do not have to change conditions? What happens is that you apply the Law, and then the conditions change spontaneously. You cannot change conditions directly—you have often tried to do so and failed—but go on the SEVEN DAY MENTAL DIET and conditions must change for you.

This then is your prescription. For seven days you must not allow yourself to dwell for a single moment on any kind of negative thought. You must watch yourself for a whole week as a cat watches a mouse, and you must not under any pretense allow your mind to dwell on any thought that is not positive, constructive, optimistic, kind. This discipline will be so strenuous that you could not maintain it consciously for much more than a week, but I do not ask you to do so. A week will be enough, because by that time the habit of positive thinking will begin to be established. Some extraordinary changes for the better will have come into your life, encouraging you enormously, and then the future will take care of itself. The new way of life will be so attractive and so much easier than the old way that you will find your mentality aligning itself almost automatically.

But the seven days are going to be strenuous. I would not have you enter upon this without counting the cost. Mere physical fasting would be child's play in comparison, even if you have a very good appetite. The most exhausting form of army gymnastics, combined with thirty mile route-marches, would be mild in comparison with this undertaking. But it is only for one week in your life, and it will definitely alter everything for the better. For the rest of your life here, for all eternity in fact, things will be utterly different and inconceivably better than if you had not carried through this undertaking.

Do not start it lightly. Think about it for a day or two before you begin. Then start in, and the grace of God go with you. You may start it any day in the week, and at any time in the day, first thing in the morning, or after breakfast, or after lunch, it does not matter, but once you do start you must go right through for the seven days. That is essential. The whole idea is to have seven days of unbroken mental discipline in order to get the mind definitely bent in a new direction once and for all.

If you make a false start, or even if you go on well for two or three days and then for any reason "fall off" the diet, the thing to do is to drop the scheme altogether for several days, and then to start again afresh. There must be no jumping on and off, as it were. You remember that Rip Van Winkle in the play would take a solemn vow of teetotalism, and then promptly accept a drink from the first neighbor who offered him one, saying calmly: "I won't count this one." Well, on the SEVEN DAY MENTAL DIET this sort of thing simply will not do. You must positively count every lapse, and whether you do or not, Nature will. Where there is a lapse you must go off the diet altogether and then start again.

Now, in order, if possible, to forestall difficulties, I will consider them in a little detail.

First of all, what do I mean by negative thinking? Well, a negative thought is any thought of failure, disappointment, or trouble; any thought of criticism, or spite, or jealousy, or condemnation of others, or self-condemnation; any thought of sickness or accident; or, in short, any kind of limitation or pessimistic thinking. Any thought that is not positive and constructive in character, whether it concerns you yourself or anyone else, is a negative thought. Do not bother too much about the question of classification, however; in practice you will never have any trouble in knowing whether a given thought is positive or negative. Even if your brain tries to deceive you, your heart will whisper the truth.

Second, you must be quite clear that what this scheme calls for is that you shall not *entertain*, or *dwell upon* negative things. Note this carefully. It is not the thoughts that come to you that matter, but only such of them as you choose to entertain and dwell upon. It does not matter what thoughts may come to you provided you do not entertain them. It is the entertaining or dwelling upon them that matters. Of course, many negative thoughts will come to you all day long. Some of them will just drift into your mind of their own accord seemingly, and these come to you out of the race mind. Other negative thoughts will be given to you by other people, either in conversation or by their conduct, or you will hear disagreeable news perhaps by letter or telephone, or you will see crimes and disasters announced in the newspaper headings. These things, however, do not matter as long as you do not entertain them. In fact, it is these very things that provide the discipline that is going to transform you during this epoch-making week. The thing to do is, directly the negative thought presents itself —turn it out. Turn away from the newspaper; turn out the thought of the unkind letter, or stupid remark, or what not. When the negative thought floats into your mind, immediately turn it out and think of something else. Best of all, think of God as explained in *The Golden Key*. A perfect analogy is furnished by the case of a man who is sitting by an open fire when a red hot cinder flies out and falls on his sleeve. If he knocks that cinder off at once, without a moment's delay to think about it, no harm is done. But if he allows it to rest on him for a single moment, under any pretense, the mischief is done, and it will be a troublesome task to repair that sleeve. So it is with a negative thought.

Now what of those negative thoughts and conditions which it is impossible to avoid at the point where you are today? What of the ordinary troubles that you will have to meet in the office or at home? The answer is, that such things will not affect your diet provided that you do not accept them, by fearing them, by believing them, by being indignant or sad about them, or by giving them any power at all. Any negative condition that duty compels you to handle will not affect your diet. Go to the office, or meet the cares at home, without allowing them to affect you. (*None of these things move me*), and all will be well. Suppose that you are lunching with a friend who talks negatively—Do not try to shut him up or otherwise snub him. Let him talk, but do not *accept* what he says, and your diet will not be affected. Suppose that on coming home you are greeted with a lot of negative conversation—do not preach a sermon, but simply do not accept it. It is your mental consent, remember, that constitutes your diet. Suppose you witness an accident or an act of injustice let us say—Instead of reacting with pity or indignation, refuse to accept the appearance at its face value; do anything that you can to right matters, give it the right thought, and let it go at that. You will still be on the diet.

Of course, it will be very helpful if you can take steps to avoid meeting during this week anyone who seems particularly likely to arouse the devil in you. People who get on your nerves, or rub you up the wrong way, or bore you, are better avoided while you are on the diet; but if it is not possible to avoid them, then you must take a little extra discipline—that is all.

Suppose that you have a particularly trying ordeal before you next week—Well, if you have enough spiritual understanding you will know how to meet that in the spiritual way; but, for our present purpose, I think I would wait and start the diet as soon as the ordeal is over. As I said before, do not take up the diet lightly, but think it over well first.

In closing, I want to tell you that people often find that the starting of this diet seems to stir up all sorts of difficulties. It seems as though everything begins to go wrong at once. This may be disconcerting, but it is really a good sign. It means that things are moving; and is not that the very object we have in view? Suppose your whole world seems to rock on its foundations. Hold on steadily, let it rock, and when the rocking is over, the picture will have reassembled itself into something much nearer to your heart's desire.

The above point is vitally important and rather subtle. Do you not see that the very dwelling upon these difficulties is in itself a negative thought which has probably thrown you off the diet? The remedy is not, of course, to deny that your world is rocking in appearance, but to refuse to take the appearance for the reality (*Judge not according to appearances but judge righteous judgment*).

A closing word of caution—Do not tell anyone else that you are on the diet, or that you intend to go on it. Keep this tremendous project strictly to yourself. Remember that your soul should be the Secret Place of the Most High. When you have come through the seven days successfully, and secured your demonstration, allow a reasonable time to elapse to establish the new mentality, and then tell the story to anyone else who you think is likely to be helped by it.

And, finally, remember that nothing said or done by anyone else can possibly throw you off the diet. Only your own reaction to the other person's conduct can do that.

Be Still

A Treatment Against Fear

Spiritual Key to Psalm XLVI

EMMET FOX

BE STILL

THE Bible teaches spiritual Truth in many different ways. It gives direct teaching about God, as clear and precise as any book on philosophy that ever was written. It expounds the Great Message indirectly through historical narrative and by means of biographical studies, for the Bible includes the most wonderful and interesting set of human biographies that ever was written. It contains an unmatched collection of essays and treatises on the nature of God and the nature of man, the powers of the soul, and the meaning of life. Consider St. John's opening section in the Gospel, for instance, or the 11th chapter of Hebrews, or the 12th and 13th of Corinthians I, or the 5th, 6th, and 7th of Matthew, to name only a few. Each of these chapters in a different way gives direct and simple teaching of the Truth, unsurpassed in any work outside of the Bible.

But it is in its prayers and treatments that the Bible is transcendent. It contains a large number of the greatest prayers ever written—beginning, of course, with what we call the "Lord's Prayer"—prayers the like of which have never been found elsewhere, for they go right down to the depths of the human soul, meeting every need that can arise, and providing for every possible temperament and any conceivable contingency—in fact they cater to "all sorts and conditions of men."

Among all the beautiful and heart searching prayers of the Bible there is none that surpasses the wonderful poem that we call the Forty-Sixth Psalm. This is an inspired treatment that will enable you to overcome any kind of difficulty; if you can tune yourself in to the level of consciousness to which it attains. It is the supreme Bible treatment against fear.

Now the object of prayer or treatment is just this very raising of the consciousness, and a good prayer is the instrument that enables us to do it. We need not expect to begin our prayer with a realization. If we already had a realization we should not be needing the help of the prayer; we do not need a step-ladder to reach a height on which we are already placed. The ladder is employed in order to enable us to raise ourselves, step by step, to a height above the ground to which our muscles alone would never carry us; and so a good prayer is a step-ladder upon which we may gradually climb from the low level of fear, doubt, and difficulty, to the spiritual height where these things melt away in the Light of Truth.

Our psalm begins, as do nearly all the Bible prayers, with an expression of faith in God. This is extremely important in practice. You need to affirm constantly that you do believe in God, not merely as a vague abstract concept, but as a real, vivid, actual power in life, always available to be contacted in thought; never changing and never failing. It cannot be too strongly emphasized that it is not sufficient to take this for granted. It is not sufficient to accept the Truth once and for all, or once a week; you must continually reaffirm it in thought, and in words if necessary. You must constantly remind yourself that you do accept this position, that you believe in it, and that your conviction is good enough to build your life and your hopes upon. All this is treatment, and very powerful treatment too. It is treatment that really changes the soul by clearing out those subconscious fears that are the cause of all your difficulties.

And so the inspired writer starts his prayer by saying, bluntly, *God is our refuge and strength, a very present help in trouble.* You will see that he allows himself no doubts at all about this. He does not dream of taking up the timid, almost apologetic, attitude that some modern divines seem to think appropriate in dealing with God. He says firmly that God IS, that He exists indeed; and then he enumerates three facts concerning God. He says that He is our refuge; he says that He is our strength; and he says that He is "a very present help in trouble." This verse is really tremendous, is it not? If we get through the crust of familiarity that tends to hide the real meaning from us, and we study these words with a fresh mind, we shall be amazed, I think, at all they imply. Note that he says that God is our refuge. He does not say that such may very well be the case, or that it is a pious hope upon which we are justified in leaning; but that, plain and plump, God is our refuge.

Now pause a moment to consider all that God is. Review briefly, at this point, the principal aspects and attributes of God as you know them, and then consider that this Infinite Being is our refuge. That is to say, this Unlimited Power of Wisdom and Love is a refuge to which we can go in any kind of difficulty. Many devout souls have thought of God as a distant potentate dwelling in the skies, to be dreaded and feared; but the Bible says on the contrary that God is a refuge for those in difficulty. It then says that his Omnipotent Power is nothing less than our strength. This brings the idea home still more vividly. God is not merely a matchless power that will come to our rescue, but He will actually be our own strength, operating through us to the overcoming of difficulty when we call upon Him in the right way.

Every student of Truth must understand that God always acts *through* us by changing our consciousness.

We learn in divine metaphysics that God never does anything *to* us, or *for* us, but always *through* us. The writer drives these points home in the familiar Bible manner by adding, "a very present help in trouble."

The opening affirmation is followed, in the most scientific way, by an excellent example of the use of what is called in metaphysics the "denial." The next two verses are a denial that there is any power in conditions to make us be, or do, or submit to, anything short of the complete all-around harmony that is the Divine Will for us all. It says *therefore will not we fear*—as following logically upon our opening affirmation —*though the earth be removed, and though the mountains be carried into the midst of the sea; Though the waters thereof roar and be troubled, though the mountains shake with the swelling thereof.*

The "earth," of course, means manifestation. It is the Bible's term for all one's manifestation, or expression—the body, home, the business life, relatives and associates, all come under the heading of the earth or the land. We know that all these outer things are but the expression of inner states of consciousness, and here the Psalmist makes us say that though the earth be removed, though all these outer things seem to go to pieces, our health break down, our money disappear, our friends desert us, yet we are not going to be afraid. This attitude is extraordinarily valuable.

When things are going wrong declare constantly that you are not going to be afraid or intimidated by any outer condition. The more afraid you find yourself, the more need is there for doing this. The most important time to say, "God is my refuge, I am not going to be afraid," is when your knees are knocking together.

The Psalmist says that though the mountains be carried into the midst of the sea, and the waters roll and tremble until the very mountains themselves seem to shake, he is not going to be afraid. The mountain, in the Bible, always means prayer, the uplifted consciousness, and this clause makes us declare that even when in the midst of our prayers things seem to get worse, so that the very prayers themselves are all but swamped by our terror, or doubt, or despair; yet we are going to hold on to the truth about God, knowing that even though it be after forty days, the water will subside—if only we hold on to the thought of God. The waters, of course, are always the human personality, and more especially the emotions.

The man who wrote this, we will agree, had no small knowledge of the human heart, its difficulties, and its needs.

There is a river, the streams whereof shall make glad the city of God, the holy place of the tabernacle of the Most High. This is the capital river mentioned several times in scripture; the river of life that flows from the throne of God. It means the understanding of Truth that is verily the "Waters of Life" to those who attain it. The river as a symbol is rather interesting. Primarily it stands for purpose. A river means purpose because it is always going somewhere. A river does not stay in one place, like a lake, or even an ocean, but is always on the way to a destination. In this respect it is a true type of the dedicated life which every student of Divine Truth is supposed to be living. In this teaching, if it really means anything to us, we are no longer drifting about like a log at the mercy of the tide, but are definitely headed along the pathway of understanding and freedom.

"The City of God" is man's consciousness. Your consciousness, which is your identity in life, is called a "city" in the Bible. "Except the Lord keep the city, the watchman waketh but in vain." Now the consciousness in which the Light of Truth begins to shine again after an attack of fear or unhappiness, is a city purified by that holy river, and it becomes a glad city, a city of God or good, a holy place for the tabernacles of the Most High. God is indeed in the midst of such a city, and when God, which is to say, our realization of God, is in the midst of our consciousness, then truly we shall not be moved.

God is in the midst of her; she shall not be moved: God shall help her, and that right early. Here the Psalmist adds one of those simple touches, expressed in the most direct and childlike language, that go straight to the heart. He says, "God shall help her—and that right early." This beautiful promise should remove the last traces of fear and doubt that may linger in the dark corners of the soul.

The metrical rhythm of the poem is preserved by a reiteration of the general theme in the next verse. *The heathen raged, the kingdoms were moved: he uttered his voice, the earth melted.* The heathen, needless to say, means your own wrong thoughts, those fears, doubts, self-reproaches, and shortcomings of every kind that come between you and your realization of God— the heathen forces that attack the holy city of your soul, sometimes lay siege to it for days and weeks, and sometimes even capture and occupy it for a time. Only for a time, however, if you hold steadfastly to God by constant prayer, for sooner or later, as surely as God lives, the kingdom of error shall be moved. He will "utter his voice" through your prayers and affirmations, and your salvation will come.

The third and last stanza of our treatment is an exercise of thanksgiving and praise. These Bible treatments are constructed with the utmost care and in the most scientific way. Usually, though not always, for there must be no hard and fast rules in prayer, they begin with an affirmation of faith in God. Then they analyze fear and worry, showing that God has no part in such things, and that we, therefore, need not fear them. They go on to remind us of the love and power and wisdom of God, and of our ability, as the children of God, to call upon His power in any kind of danger or trouble. They make these truths vivid to us with unexcelled literary skill, using the most diverse images and examples to that end; and then they commonly finish, as prayers nearly always should, with a song of praise and thanksgiving.

Now the Psalmist makes us say *The Lord of hosts is with us: the God of Jacob is our refuge.* This destroys the feeling of God being afar off. The "Lord of Hosts" is the title for God that stresses His great power and might. It is the *omnipotence* aspect of God, we should say technically. So here we declare that Omnipotence is with us, and working through us; and he carefully adds that It is also the God of Jacob. Now Jacob stands for the soul that is not yet redeemed, the soul still struggling in difficulty and conscious imperfection. Israel, "the Prince of God," is the soul that has realized its divine nature; but Jacob is still in the midst of his troubles. So the Psalmist here reminds us that God is the Great Power, the Lord of Hosts, for Jacob just as well as for Israel.

Come, behold the works of the Lord, what

desolations he hath made in the earth. He maketh wars to cease unto the end of the earth; he breaketh the bow, and cutteth the spear in sunder; he burneth the chariot in the fire. Here he continues with thanksgiving, saying, in effect: Let us consider the power and the glory of this God who is always with us; how his action in prayer transforms our conditions, and makes desolate, or destroys, our troubles and worries; how He makes the wars—a splendid name for that worrying and stewing in misery that blights the lives of so many people—to cease in every part of our consciousness; how he disarms all the things of which we are afraid, not just putting them out of the way for the time being, but absolutely destroying any power they ever had. When you captured an enemy regiment in those days, smashed their bows and their spears, and burned their chariots, you had put them out of action pretty completely. That regiment could never trouble you again.

Be still and know that I am God: I will be exalted among the heathen, I will be exalted in the earth. This really is probably the most wonderful phrase in the whole Bible. It really is the whole Bible in a nutshell. "Be still, and know that I am God." This is just the very last thing that we want to do when we are worried or anxious. The current of human thought that Paul calls the carnal mind is hurrying us along to its own ends, and it seems much easier to swim with it by accepting difficulties, by rehearsing grievances, by dwelling upon symptoms, than to draw resolutely away in thought from these things, and contemplate God, which is the one way out of trouble.

Train yourself to rise above this hurrying tide of error—error is always hurried; to sweep you off your feet is its master strategy—and, turning your back upon conditions, however bad they may seem, *be still and know that I am God.*

Even in your prayers there is a time for vigorous treatment, and there is also a time to cease active work and, "having done all, to stand"—to *be still and know that I am God.*

This of course does not mean merely doing nothing, or going away to concern one's self with some secular thing such as reading a novel or a newspaper. It is being still *to know that God is God.* Such "stillness" is the reverse of laziness or inaction. The still dwelling upon God is the quietest but the most potent action of all.

The Lord of hosts is with us; the God of Jacob is our refuge. Here again metrical symmetry obliges the poet to close his wonderful poem with a repetition of the general theme. Spiritually, too, it is a most powerful and effective ending to our prayer. The God of power who helps weak and frail mortals in the day of trouble is working through us, and so all will be well.

Note: The word *Selah* is no part of the poem itself but a stage direction to the temple musicians who chanted the psalms as part of the liturgy.

The Wonder Child

STRANGE as it may seem to you, there exists a mystic power that is able to transform your life so thoroughly, so radically, so completely, that when the process is completed your own friends would hardly recognize you, and in fact you would scarcely be able to recognize yourself. You would sit down and ask yourself: "Can I really be the man or woman that I vaguely remember, who went about under my name six months or six years ago? Was I really that person? Could that person possibly have been I?" And the truth will be that while in one sense you are indeed the same person, yet in another sense you will be someone utterly different. This mystic but intensely real force can pick you up today, *now*, from the midst of failure, ruin, misery, despair—and in the twinkling of an eye, as St. Paul said, solve your problems, smooth out your difficulties, cut you free from any entanglements, and place you clear, safe, and happy upon the highroad of freedom and opportunity.

It can lift you out of an invalid's bed, make you sound and well once more, and free to go out into the world to shape your life as you will. It can throw open the prison door and liberate the captive. It has a magical healing balm for the bruised or broken heart.

This mystic Power can teach you all things that you need to know, if only you are receptive and teachable. It can inspire you with new thoughts and ideas, so that your work may be truly original. It can impart new and wonderful kinds of knowledge as soon as you really want such knowledge—glorious knowledge—strange things not taught in schools or written in books. It can do for you that which is probably the most important thing of all in your present stage: it can find your true place in life for you, and put you into it too. It can find the right friends for you, kindred spirits who are interested in the same ideas and want the same things that you do. It can provide you with an ideal home. It can furnish you with the prosperity that means freedom, freedom to be and to do and to go as your soul calls.

This extraordinary Power, mystic though I have rightly called it, is nevertheless very real, no mere imaginary abstraction, but actually the most practical thing there is. The existence of this Power is already well known to thousands of people in the world today, and has been known to certain enlightened souls for tens of thousands of years. This Power is really no less than the primal Power of Being, and to discover that Power is the divine birthright of all men. It is your right and your privilege to make your contact with this Power, and to allow it to work through your body, mind, and estate, so that you need no longer grovel upon the ground amid limitations and difficulties, but can soar up on wings like an eagle to the realm of dominion and joy.

But where, it will naturally be asked, is this wonderful, Mystic Power to be contacted? Where may we find it? and how is it brought into action? The answer is perfectly simple—This Power is to be found within your own consciousness, the last place that most people would look for it. Right within your own mentality there lies a source of energy stronger than electricity, more potent than high explosive; unlimited and inexhaustible. You only need to make conscious contact with this Power to set it working in your affairs; and all the marvelous results enumerated can be yours. This is the real meaning of such sayings in the Bible as "The Kingdom of God is within you"; and "Seek ye first the Kingdom of God, and all the rest shall be added."

This Indwelling Power, the Inner Light,

or Spiritual Idea, is spoken of in the Bible as a child, and throughout the scriptures the child symbolically always stands for this. Bible symbolism has its own beautiful logic, and just as the soul is always spoken of as a woman, so this, the Spiritual Idea that is born to the soul, is described as a child. The conscious discovery by you that you have this Power within you, and your determination to make use of it, is the birth of the child. And it is easy to see how very apt the symbol is, for the infant that is born in consciousness is just such a weak, feeble entity as any new-born child, and it calls for the same careful nursing and guarding that any infant does in its earliest days. After a time, however, as the weeks go by, the child grows stronger and bigger, until a time comes when it can well take care of itself; and then it grows and grows in wisdom and stature until, no longer leaning on the mother's care, the child, now arrived at man's estate, turns the tables, and repays its debt by taking over the care of its mother. So your ability to contact the mystic Power within yourself, frail and feeble at first, will gradually develop until you find yourself permitting that Power to take your whole life into its care.

The life story of Jesus, the central figure of the Bible, perfectly dramatizes this truth. He is described as being born of a virgin, and in a poor stable, and we know how he grew up to be the Saviour of the world. Now, in Bible symbolism, the virgin soul means the soul that looks to God alone, and it is this condition of soul in which the child, or Spiritual Idea, comes to birth. It is when we have reached that stage, the stage where, either through wisdom or because of suffering, we are prepared to put God really first, that the thing happens.

The Christ Child was born in a stable, though all the world had anticipated that when He arrived it would be in a palace;

and we deeply appreciate the significance of this point as soon as the Holy Child comes to birth in our own soul, for with the natural consciousness of our own unworthiness we feel only too keenly that once more He is indeed being born in a stable. Here we have the inspired intimation that this fact will not prevent His growing up to be the saviour of our own individual world.

The Bible directly and indirectly has a good deal to say on the subject of the birth and growth of the child, and what it can mean for us. One of the most significant pronouncements on this subject is given in the Book of Isaiah, chapter 9, verses 2,6, and 7, and it will amply repay us to consider that statement in some detail.

Isaiah says: "The people that walked in darkness have seen a great light: they that dwell in the land of the shadow of death, upon them hath the light shined." This is a marvelous description of what happens when the Spiritual Idea, the child, is born to the soul. Walking in darkness, moral or physical, dwelling in the land of the shadow of death—the death of joy, or hope, or even self-respect—describes well the condition of many people before this light shines into their weary, heartbroken lives; and the Prophet rises into a paean of exultant joy as he contemplates the deliverance wrought by the mystic Power: "For unto us a child is born, unto us a son is given: and the government shall be upon his shoulder: and his name shall be called Wonderful, Counsellor, The mighty God, The everlasting Father, The Prince of Peace."

This description begins by giving the gist of the whole matter, simply and concisely —that the government is to be upon *his* shoulder. This really covers the whole business. Correctly understood, this statement tells the entire story without need of any further comment. It means that once you have contacted the mystic Power within, and have allowed it to take over your responsibilities for you, it will direct and govern all your affairs from the greatest to the least without trouble to you. *The government shall be upon his shoulder.* You are tired, and driven, and worried, and weak, and ill, and depressed, because you have been trying to carry the government upon your own shoulder; the burden is too much for you, and you have broken down under it. Now, immediately you hand over your self-government, that is the burden of making a living, or of healing your body, or erasing your mistakes, to the Child, He, the Tireless One, the All-Powerful, the All-Wise, the All-Resourceful, assumes it with joy; and your difficulties have seen the beginning of the end.

The Prophet next goes on to speak of the "Name" of the child, and if we know something of Bible symbolism, we know that we are now going to learn something fundamental, for in the Bible, the *Name* of anything, means the character or nature of that thing, and so we realize that a name is not merely an arbitrary label, but actually a hieroglyph of the soul. We are given no less than five names or qualities of the child. Let us examine them and see what they tell us. First of all, Isaiah says that the name of the child is Wonderful, and this in fact is the first and the outstanding quality; this child is a Wonder Child. The word "wonderful" used here requires to be carefully scrutinized. As employed in the Bible, it implies simply and plainly a miracle; —a miracle, just that, and nothing less, because you have to realize that the Bible teaches the miracle from the first page to the last. The Bible repeatedly says that miracles can happen, and that they do happen; and it gives detailed and circumstantial accounts of many specific cases. And it says, many times, that miracles always will happen if you believe them to be possible, and are willing to recognize the Power of God, and to call upon it.

There have been many efforts during the last two generations to divorce the Bible teaching from the belief in miracles. Attempts have been made to show that in some unexplained way the Bible can be true and useful, and yet mistaken in its teaching of the miracle; in other words, that it can in some mysterious manner be an edifying conglomeration of truth and lies. Indeed, one famous Bible critic said blandly: "Miracles do not happen"—thus dismissing the whole matter with a wave of his hand. The obvious rejoinder to this is that if it were true that miracles do not happen, the Bible would be a mere meaningless jumble of pointless fables. But they do happen, and even as Galileo terminated the other controversy by saying, "nevertheless it revolves," so when all controversy finishes, we may say of miracles "nevertheless, they happen."

Well now, just recollect the first quality that Isaiah gives for the child. It is a *wonder* child; that is to say, it is a miraculous child; it is a worker of miracles. This means that as soon as the Wonder Child is born in your consciousness, the miracle will come into your life—a real miracle, remember. This does not mean simply that you will become resigned to your present circumstances, or merely that you will then be enabled to meet the same difficulties with a higher courage or a clearer brain. It means the *miracle*. It means that the Wonder Child, not in any figurative or metaphorical sense, but plainly and literally, in the most matter-of-fact meaning of the term, will work miracles in your life. It will do these things absolutely, irrespective of what your present conditions are. It is in no way constrained or constricted by your present circumstances. The whole point is that the Wonder Child can lift you out of those very circumstances, and set you down in different circumstances. The Wonder Child is the Miracle Child.

Now let us take the second point that the Prophet gives us concerning this Wonder Child. He calls it "Counsellor," and a counsellor, you know, is one who gives advice or guidance; and so you see that once the Child has been born, you need never again lack either of these things. The Child will be your infallible counsellor. If you are worried because you do not know whether or not to take some important step, to accept or reject a business offer, to sign or not to sign an important document, to enter upon or to dissolve a partnership, to resign your position or not, to go abroad or to stay at home, to trust someone or not to trust him, to say something or to leave it unsaid, the Wonder Child will be your Counsellor, and the Wonder Child is never mistaken.

It is in the third point that the Prophet reveals to us who the Wonder Child really is. It is no less than God Himself, "The Mighty God," as Isaiah reminds us, and truly the mystic Power that transforms, and transmutes, and transfigures, is *God Himself*, always present with you, and always available, once you have understood and accepted the Spiritual Idea. And it is because He is God, that the work of the Child is independent of all conditions.

The fourth name that the Prophet attributes to the Child is that of Everlasting Father. This point establishes our relationship to God in unmistakable terms. As Jesus so clearly pointed out, God is our Father, not merely our Creator, and we as the children of a good Father may expect to find ourselves provided with everything that we need for body and soul. But since we have to establish for ourselves our own consciousness of this fact, and as our demonstration is just the measure of our understanding of it, our concept of the divine fact is the fruit of our own soul, and may mystically be called our child.

Finally, in the fifth point, we receive what is perhaps the greatest name of all. Here the Child is called "The Prince of Peace." Just try to realize a little what this title must mean for you in practice—nothing less than that the Wonder Child, the Spiritual Idea, born to your own soul, is the Prince of Peace. Now think what perfect peace of soul, if you could attain it, would actually mean to you. If your soul were truly at peace, what in your life could go wrong? If only you had real peace of soul, do you suppose that your body could be ill? Given real peace of soul, how easy it would be to find your true place in the world, which would mean prosperity as well as happiness. How easily, how quickly and efficiently you could perform your work, work such as you have never done yet, and in less than half the usual time. Of course, everybody knows that this is what would follow the attainment of soul peace, but there is still much more in it than that. What you perhaps do not know is that once you have attained true peace of soul, you have made it possible for the Mystic Power, the Wonder Child, to teach you new things, utterly beyond the compass of your present understanding, enabling you to do things in the world, if you should wish to, that nobody would have deemed it possible that you could do. Well, it is in the very nature of the Wonder Child to give you just that very soul peace, and it is because of this function that it is called "The Prince of Peace".

Isaiah goes on to tell us that this is no limited demonstration, but that once it begins, it goes on and on as we rise higher and higher in consciousness, increasing and expanding more and more unto the perfect day. "Of the increase of his government and peace there shall be no end, upon the throne of David, and upon his kingdom, to order it, and to establish it with judgment and with justice from henceforth even forever." The throne of David is of course Jerusalem, which is Uru-Salem, the city of peace, this very peace that we have been discussing; and Jerusalem symbolically is the awakened consciousness. There shall indeed be no end to the increase of *that* government, and in view of the possibility that the weaker souls, the fearful, and the unbelieving, and the depressed, should find it impossible to believe that such good tidings could possibly be true, the Prophet clinches the matter with the definite assertion: "The Zeal of the Lord of Hosts will perform this." This should remove all sense of personal responsibility for the demonstration, the bugbear of so many seekers. Have we not seen that the gist of the whole matter is just this very point—that the government shall be upon *his* shoulder.

DANIEL IN THE LIONS' DEN

THE story of Daniel in the lions' den is one of the half dozen best known stories in the Bible. I imagine there are very few people who have not heard it. It is a particular favorite with the children, and children are great judges of literary and dramatic power, as every one knows who has ever tried to entertain one of them with a story. Now we learn from the Jesus Christ teaching that there is no such thing as chance. Everything happens in accordance with the law of cause and effect, and, therefore, when a story or a legend is found to have a world-wide circulation, and when that circulation continues generation after generation, we know that it must contain something of great importance to humanity. So it is with the story of Daniel's great demonstration. It contains within it a wonderful lesson in the Truth of Being, and for all these centuries it has helped and comforted millions of people, even though they did not have the scientific key to its meaning.

DANIEL IN THE LIONS' DEN

Let us now consider in a little detail some of the principal points of the story as it is given in the 6th Chapter of Daniel. We are told that Daniel was made what would be called nowadays Chancellor, or chief Secretary of State, under Darius. This was a position of great honor and responsibility, but also one involving great personal danger to the holder. One could not occupy such an office without making many powerful enemies, and in that ancient Oriental world they were apt to make short work of inconvenient officials in high places, more particularly when the incumbent was a foreigner. The sword or dagger, poison administered in food, and even through wearing apparel such as gloves or boots, were freely employed in such cases, and, above all, political intrigue was used to bring the obnoxious official to his end.

In the case of Daniel we are told that a carefully engineered plot was carried through, which placed his patron, Darius, in the position of being absolutely helpless to save Daniel. Such plotters would take the character of the monarch into account when laying their plans. A small-

DANIEL IN THE LIONS' DEN

minded, jealous man would be handled in one way, a religious fanatic in another. Darius, who was neither of these things, but an intellectual formalist of a rigid type, was trapped in his own weakness. Daniel was arrested, taken down to a pit of lions, and thrown in. Such a pit of wild animals was sure to be found near most Eastern palaces of those days, the animals being required partly for display, and partly, as in the present instance, to furnish terrifying examples of political punishment. Daniel, however, instead of being promptly torn to pieces, remained untouched, and in due course was liberated from the lions' den without so much as a scratch.

Spiritually understood this is one of the greatest lessons in the Bible. Daniel is Everyman. The story of his great tribulation is the story of any difficulty that can come into your life, or into mine. Incidentally, it is the story of the whole of your human experience in general, but it applies also to each individual difficulty that you have to overcome. Remember that every individual problem that you have to face is but a tiny model, as it were, of the great problem

DANIEL IN THE LIONS' DEN

of overcoming our human belief in limitation, sickness, sin, and death, that is called in theology the Fall of Man.

When some great problem or trouble comes into your life you are, figuratively speaking, thrown into a pit of lions, and many fearful hearts have felt that this is indeed a very graphic description of the state of mind they have experienced.

Now let us look for the key to the story and we shall find it here in Verse 10. *Daniel had acquired the habit of prayer.* Daniel was a man who practised the Presence of God, not now and again, but constantly and regularly. This verse is very illuminating. We are told that Daniel knew that the warrant for his arrest was signed. (When you are working and praying regularly, along the right lines, you will always get to know anything which it is necessary that you should know; you will not be taken by surprise.) Daniel knew that trouble was pending, and immediately he started praying, or treating about it. He did not pronounce an affirmation once or twice and expect it to work, like an incantation.

DANIEL IN THE LIONS' DEN

He prayed, clearing up his consciousness, three times a day. *"His windows being open in his chamber toward Jerusalem."* Of course the "chamber" is the "secret place" of Jesus, or one's consciousness. Jerusalem is always the highest part of man's nature or personality, short of the actual realization of God; and so Daniel, three times a day, turned in thought to God and raised his thought as high as he possibly could. No one can do more than this. It is a mistake to think that you must get a wonderfully vivid realization of Spirit in order to overcome any difficulty. Prayer will get you out of your difficulty whether you get any realization or not. You can always open your window toward Jerusalem. Whether you ascend Mount Zion, which is the realization of God Himself, does not lie in your hands—the turning toward Jerusalem does.

In the same verse it says *"as he did aforetime."* This tells us that Daniel was in the habit of thus praying scientifically. Some people pray only when they are in trouble, and then, naturally they do not find it easy to get any sort of contact. One would not expect to practise on the piano only occasionally, and yet play well on any desired occasion. Daniel made a regular practice of prayer and meditation three times a day, and when the dark hour came, this practice stood by him. He knew beforehand that trouble was coming. He probably knew almost exactly what it would be. And he met it by working steadily on his own consciousness in order to get rid of fear. He probably succeeded in doing this even before his arrest, and was able to rejoice in victory well before the victory itself made its appearance.

Of course, the real causes of all our troubles lie within ourselves. The only enemies we have to overcome in the long run are our own fears, doubts, selfishness, and so forth. These are typified by King Darius and the plotters. All your enemies are within yourself—*"a man's enemies shall be those of his own household."* Darius represents, in particular, our belief in the power of the external world to limit or injure us. He represents none of the things that are usually called evil, but rather our limiting belief in the fixed and unchangeable character of outer things that are in themselves good.

The truth is that no outer conditions have any power in themselves, no outer laws need bind us, when we appeal to the supreme Christ Law of divine freedom and harmony; but we do not know, or we forget this great truth, and so we go on believing in and submitting to all kinds of supposed laws of limitation. We believe that we are too old to do something that we could very well do. We believe that a certain climate can adversely affect our bodies, when in truth it has no such power. I knew a man in London who was working for the municipal government, a service which is swathed in red tape and vexatious restrictions of every kind. Feeling this fact acutely, he remained in a subordinate position for three years through being under the impression that his qualifications did not admit him to a certain higher grade, the work of which he knew he could do very well. After these three years he learned accidentally that there was in fact no regulation such as he had supposed to prevent his holding such a position, and he promptly applied for it, and was appointed, with a considerable increase in salary. This is an example of a belief in an outer limitation which in reality could have been overcome at any moment. It is a good example of Darius. The supposed rule concerning qualifications was not. even supposedly, an evil thing like dishonesty, deceit, or murder, but a rule, good in intention, to insure the appointment of suitable people.

The plotters represent essentially evil things, such as the above mentioned sins, and of course Everyman has to reckon with these too. *"The law of the Medes and Persians, which altereth not,"* is a splendid expression of our usual notion of these outer limitations as being impossible to overcome, of there being things and conditions that we just have to "put up with."

There is a well known picture of Daniel in the Lions' Den, which was certainly painted by an inspired artist. Most of my readers will know it, and I always keep a copy of it in my room. Daniel is shown *not looking at the lions,* but turning his back on them! What a lesson in scientific prayer or treatment; what I have elsewhere called "the Golden Key." The more we think over any difficulty the more we amplify it, and staring at our lions causes them to grow and grow until they are as big as elephants. Daniel is shown looking upward toward the light—a graphic representation of the Practice of the Presence—and the lions, instead of looking ferocious or angry, seem good humored enough as they stroll about or stand watching him curiously.

Those who have had much to do with wild animals in their native jungle always insist that no wild animal will attack a man who is not afraid of it. In India many stories are told of true Yogis (that is those who follow the Rajah or royal Yoga which is the search for reunion with God, and not just the acquiring of the power to play tricks on the etheric plane) living among tigers and other beasts of prey in perfect safety, and the Bible itself tells us that a time will come when the lion shall lie down with the lamb, because man has gotten fear, and hatred, and jealousy, and condemnation out of his own heart, and has thereby changed the whole moral and spiritual climate of this planet.

When you are in trouble you are Daniel in the Lions' Den. The lions will seem terribly ferocious; but pray until fear has begun to go; keep knowing the Truth, in the face of all appearances; and you will come out of the lions' den safe and sound, without a single scratch, as Daniel did. Nay more—you will come out stronger and better for the ordeal, because no problem that we meet in the light of Truth ever leaves us where it found us. Every problem thus overcome is a definite step upward in the growth of the soul.

It is significant, is it not, that being unable to accuse Daniel of any of the ordinary transgressions, his enemies proved beyond a shadow of doubt that Daniel was a man who declined to worship (to believe in or trust) any power but GOD. In the sight of the world this was an indictable offense, but in the light of Truth it was shown to be Daniel's salvation.

The longer one continues in the Truth teaching the more convinced he becomes of the fact that this is a mental world, and that man's dominion lies within his own mentality. When once we have grasped this fact clearly and have determined to put it into operation in our lives, it seems as though our difficulties were over, and theoretically this could be the case. Practically, however, it calls for the most rigid and persistent watchfulness on our part, if we are not to be constantly straying from the true path of correct thought. "Watch and pray," said Jesus, knowing how subtle are the temptations to step aside into old errors. "The price of liberty is eternal vigilance," said an ancient sage, and never was this truer than in the life of the soul.

If you really want to demonstrate health, happiness, and true prosperity—and every student of Truth knows that it is his duty to demonstrate these things as soon as he possibly can—you must set aside a definite time every day for prayer and meditation, and for checking up upon your own daily conduct and demonstration, or want of demonstration. You must conduct the affairs of your soul in a business-like way.

Too many religious people fail to realize that the business of spiritual growth calls for order, method, and intelligent organization, just as much as does any commercial business or engineering enterprise, or any other important activity, if it is to be a success.*

So great is the power of prayer that not only will it get you out of any difficulty, but the things in yourself which produced that difficulty will be utterly destroyed forever, with all their associated thoughts and fears; and all consequences or collateral effects that might arise from the problem itself will be taken care of too—*"and brake all their bones in pieces or ever they came at the bottom of the den."*

There is no end to a prayer. It echoes on forever in your soul. Long after the visible demonstration has been made and forgotten, the prayer that produced it continues to work for your spiritual advancement, for the creative power of a God thought is unlimited and eternal.

*The Fifteen Points card should be studied on this subject (see back of book).

FAITH

Faith is the substance of things hoped for, the evidence of things not seen.
For by it the elders obtained a good report.
—Hebrews 11:1-2

THERE is a good deal of misconception among students of Truth upon the subject of Faith. Some of those who are on the Spiritual Basis confuse the idea of Faith with the conventional type of faith healing which always fades into disrepute sooner or later because it cannot be relied upon to give steady results. Nevertheless, Faith, properly understood is a necessary part of every demonstration.

The confusion arises because *blind* Faith is not really Faith at all, but quite a different thing; namely, Hope. Now Hope is not of the slightest use in demonstrations—frail, anaemic, unfruitful in results, she it is who maketh the heart sick. It is her elder sister, Faith, who is the *substance,* the evidence, the sure and certain forerunner of victory. This is so because Faith properly under-

FAITH

stood is the result of the understanding of Principle. When we have an adequate understanding of the true nature of being, we have Faith that the Law, properly applied, cannot and will not fail us; and so, when a practical problem presents itself, a call for healing or supply, perhaps, a sound comprehension of this Law produces the scientific conviction, and then the demonstration necessarily follows. Thus it is the Elders, those in the possession of spiritual understanding, who receive the true report or demonstration.

The New Testament, among many other things, is a healer's case book, and in most of the instances cited, Faith was regarded as being a necessary preliminary — *"Stretch forth Thy hand."* The essential doctrine on the subject is presented in the dramatic episode of the withering of the fig tree. The Master was desirous of proving to his students the power of understanding thought. For this reason he destroyed the fig tree. He naturally would not select an animal for this purpose, and a mineral would have been useless. A plant was the proper thing to experiment upon.

FAITH

The following day the Disciples were amazed to discover that the tree against which the word had been spoken was destroyed. Upon calling his attention to this, he said in effect—"Yes, and that shows you the power of trained thought —you are surprised at this, but I tell you that you could order that mountain itself to be thrown into the sea, and it would happen, if you really believed it, and did not doubt in your hearts." Then he added significantly—"before you practise the power of the word, if you are not at peace with everybody, treat yourself until you are."* This episode is so dramatic and so outstanding once we understand the nature of thought, that we are astonished that the world could have missed it so long.

The closing incident is particularly notable— he warned them of hostile or critical thoughts, *because of the harm they would do to themselves.* Many people are greatly afraid of other people's thoughts, but there is no need for any such fear.

Nothing can come into your experience unless it first enters your mentality, and nothing can

*Matthew 21:19. Mark 11:12-14; 20-26.

enter your mentality unless it there finds something like itself to which it can attach itself. As long as your heart is really clear of ill-will, you are perfectly safe. On the other hand, the use of the power of thought in hostility to others could only result in very severe suffering and punishment for yourself. According to your belief is it done unto you. To think evil of Tom, Dick, or Harry, is to think evil; and to think evil, *ipso facto,* is to call it down upon yourself.

There are many who appreciate the power of Faith, but lament that they do not possess it, and fear that because of this they can make no progress in Truth. There is no need for such apprehension. The Will to Faith in itself constitutes Faith, for the purpose of a metaphysical act or treatment, and is sufficient. Dissociate yourself from your own doubts. Remove your consent, and they lose all power. You are not your mind—you are not your thoughts—you are not your doubts. Say: "Yes, my mind is full of doubts, but *I* am not. I am not consenting to it—I have spoken the word, and it shall not return void." This is the substance of the thing you hope for. It is the evidence of the thing not seen. No power can hinder it.

The Zodiac and the Bible
The End of the World

THERE has recently been still another revival of the talk about the end of the world. Once again newspaper articles are being written and public meetings held, both in America and in Great Britain, where more or less sensational statements are made to the effect that the end of the world is now due, and may be expected at any moment. Ever since the outbreak of the Great War in 1914 the prophets have been exceptionally busy in this direction, and on several occasions groups of people have actually sat up all night waiting for the end.

Now the old adage says that there is no smoke without fire, and it proves itself in the present instance, for behind all this speculation and discussion a great truth undoubtedly does lie, and in this booklet I propose to explain exactly what it is.

The actual fact is that, while it is not true that the end of the world in the ordinary sense of the words is coming upon us, we do indeed stand on the threshold of a new age. One age has now passed away and another age is coming into being, and it is this tremendous change in the unfoldment of the human race that people of all sorts everywhere have been sensing. In other words, humanity is now entering upon a new era in its history, and this means that most of the old ideas in which we were all brought up are now definitely become out of date, and that we shall have to adapt ourselves to a completely new outlook upon life. A completely new outlook, mark you—no mere rearrangement of old ideas into a new pattern, such as the changing of a monarchy into a republic or a republic into a monarchy, the disestablishing of one church and the establishing of a rival one, the swapping of King Log for King Stork, or the changing of Tweedledum for Tweedledee. It means a complete change in all our fundamental values, a completely new way of looking at all human problems—in fact a new age.

Many people are looking about them today with a feeling of consternation at what they see in the world. Old landmarks, like the Austrian Empire, the Czarist Empire, the Hohenzollern Empire, and the Turkish Empire, are swept away within four short years. The ancient Chinese Empire in the East and the Spanish Monarchy in the West have disappeared too. The greatest material boom in recorded history has been followed by the greatest depression. The Governor of the Bank of England has publicly stated that after months of investigation he does not understand the causes of the depression, and that he has no remedy to offer for dealing with it. The orthodox churches were once hardly adequate to meet the needs of a smaller population, and now churchmen complain of the empty pews that face them Sunday after Sunday; and the reason is that the old theological sanctions which once meant so much are no longer taken seriously by the great masses of the people. In fact, it is often said bitterly that nothing is as it was; everything is changed. General Smuts said a year or two ago, "Humanity has once more struck its tents, and is again on the march."

All this is perfectly correct, as far as it goes, but when once we have the key to the main-spring of human history we shall no longer be either surprised or dismayed at these occurrences. No matter what the next few years may hold—and beyond a doubt they are going to show us some very surprising things—we shall not be either alarmed or grieved if we realize what it is that is really happening.

The history of mankind proceeds in no haphazard or casual way, but through the unfoldment of a number of distinct periods or ages. Each of these periods has its own characteristics, its own lessons to be learned, its own work to be done; and each one is quite fundamentally different in every respect from its predecessor and not a mere improvement or expansion of it. Each of these ages lasts approximately two thousand years; to be more precise, each one is usually about two thousand, one hundred and fifty years long; and the passing from one such age into another is always accompanied by both external and internal storm and stress such as the world has recently been going through. The last change took place a couple of thousand years ago, and the new world that formed itself from that melting pot was the western Christian civilization that we know. This great enterprise having worked itself out and fulfilled its mission, has now drawn to its close, and the new age is already upon us.

In connection with the coming and going of these different ages it is necessary to be familiar with the natural phenomenon known as the Precession of the Equinoxes. It is not necessary that a student should possess any general knowledge of astronomy; it is sufficient to know that as we look out from our globe at the illimitable starry hosts that surround us, the axis of the earth seems to trace out a huge circle in the heavens every twenty-six thousand years or thereabouts. This huge circle, which is known as the Zodiac, falls into twelve parts or sectors, and each part, or "Sign," as the Ancients called it, marks the passage of time that we occupy in working through one of our "Ages."

This "Zodiac" is one of the most interesting of all the symbols that reveal the destiny of mankind. In fact, the Zodiac with its twelve signs, symbolizes the most fundamental thing in the nature of man. It is nothing less than the key to the history of the Human Race, of the psychology of the individual man, and of his regeneration or spiritual salvation. The Bible, which is of course the great fountain of

THE ZODIAC AND THE BIBLE

Truth, has the Zodiac running through it from beginning to end. The twelve sons of Jacob who become the twelve tribes of the Old Testament, and the twelve Apostles of the New Testament, are, apart from their historical identity, special expressions of the twelve signs of the Zodiac. The marshalling of the Twelve Tribes of Israel in strict astronomical order in the great encampment of the wilderness is a leading example of this Zodiacal symbolism which the reader can check for himself.

The knowledge of this mysterious thing, the Zodiac. is found all over the world, among all races, and in all ages. Excavations among the most ancient ruins in Asia have revealed representations of the Zodiac. Both the earlier and the later Egyptians understood it well. The Chaldæans were masters of the subject. It was engraved upon the temples of Greece and Rome. The American aborigines in Mexico and Peru were well acquainted with it; the oldest Chinese records speak of it; and it has turned up unexpectedly on forgotten islands in the Pacific. Pythagoras taught it in the olden days, of course; and it was incorporated into the fabric of more than one of the mediaeval cathedrals. The Great Circle at Stonehenge is really a type of the Zodiac; and the twelve Signs, beautifully executed, form part of the ornamentation of several of the very newest and highest skyscrapers in New York.

Now what is the real significance of the Zodiac

which so universally permeates all human culture? It is a curious and most interesting fact that men constantly employ, and thus perpetuate, symbols of whose real meaning they are not consciously aware. Often in this way the profoundest truths are enshrined in what seems to be but a casual ornamentation.

The Zodiac has usually been either ignored, or treated as a mere picturesque decoration, or else it has been degraded into superstition and fortune telling; and so we have now to ask ourselves the question—What is the real significance of the Zodiac? And in order to answer that question we must put another one—What is the real reason of mankind being on the earth at all? What are we here for? What is it all about? Why are we born, and why do we die? Is there a reason or a pattern behind it all? And if so, what is it? And the answer to these questions, no doubt the most fundamental of all questions, is this: That we are here to learn the Truth of Being. That we are here to become self-conscious, self-governed entities, focal points of the Divine Mind, each expressing God in a new way. That is the object of our existence, and the only thing that we have to do to realize it is to get a better knowledge of God, because such knowledge is the answer to every problem. All trouble, all sin, sickness, poverty, accidents, death itself, are due simply to a want of knowledge of

God, and, per contra, all health, success, prosperity, beauty, joy and happiness consist in obtaining that knowledge of God. When we are in trouble of any kind it means that for the time being our knowledge of God is inadequate; and recovery means that our knowledge of God has become clearer.

Of course, some individuals progress far more rapidly than the main bulk. These are the leaders and teachers of the race. But the main body of humanity is always steadily, if it may seem a little slowly, growing in its knowledge of God. This is the reality behind what we call progress, or evolution. The passage from savagery to barbarism, and from barbarism on to civilization is really a growth in the knowledge of God. All the things that we see as scientific, artistic, or social advancement; such diverse things as the spread of hygiene, universal and compulsory education, the abolition of slavery, and the emancipation of women; all these things are really but the outer expression of mankind's increase in the true knowledge of God.

In order to acquire that full understanding of all that God is, that full understanding which will be his complete salvation, man has to learn, piecemeal as it were, to know God in twelve different ways. It takes him a couple of thousand years to learn each of these lessons; and so, we can, if we like, think of our progress around the Zodiac as a series of twelve lessons which we have to learn about

God. We have now finished our last lesson, and have already begun our study of the new one.

Each of these lessons has a name which has been allotted to it for convenience. Everything must have a name, but, as many of us know, names when rightly understood are often found to be symbolical of the things for which they stand, and the names of our lessons or "Signs" are no exception to this rule. The name of the last sign, the one which we have just left, was Pisces, or the Fishes. The one before that, which we left over two thousand years ago, was Aries, or the Ram. The one before that was Taurus, or the Bull, and so forth. These names, be it noted, do not in the least refer to the physical shape of the constellations as seen in the sky—much effort has been wasted in the endeavor to trace a far-fetched resemblance to a lion, or a bull, or a centaur, where there is not the very faintest ground for so doing—they refer to the innate character of the lesson that we have to learn at the particular time that is indicated by the Sign.

The new age upon which we have now entered is called Aquarius—the Man with the Water Pot—and the Aquarian Age is going to be a completely new chapter in the history of mankind. The student should be very clear about this. A new age means everything new, and not just a polishing up of the old Piscean ideas which most people make the mistake of regarding as the only possible ideas

—the only natural and established order of things—instead of being merely one of an infinite number of possible expressions.

As a matter of fact, we are, within the not very far distant future, going to change everything in the outer world around us. Our political, social, and ecclesiastical institutions, our methods of doing our daily work, our relationships with one another, our manifold instruments of self-expression and self-discovery—all will undergo a change, a radical change, and for the better. A few of these changes have already come about, but the really big changes are yet to be.

Now, concerning these changes, it will be the attitude which the individual adopts towards them which will determine their reaction upon him. If we take up an attitude of resistance to these natural changes, if we, so to say, antagonize them in our own consciousness, if we assume that change must necessarily be bad—which is only another way of saying that all our present arrangements are perfect and unimprovable—then we shall suffer a sense of conflict, and defeat, and loss. We shall go about saying, "the country is going to the dogs"; talk foolishly about "the good old days" (which never existed); and, in fact, take up the stock attitude of obscurantism and reaction. Our soul will become, what was said of a certain university, "a home of lost causes and dead faiths." And all this will mean, temporarily, at least, defeat, failure, and waste.

If, on the other hand, we know the Truth and practise it, we shall sweep forward in the grand march of humanity, learning the new lesson, rejoicing in the new work, and triumphing in its triumphs. If, instead of seeking to hold on to the wreckage of outworn things, we are prepared to march breast forward and, as has been finely said, "greet the unknown with a cheer," then indeed shall we be loyal servants of God and of our fellow men. The summing up of all wisdom is also the fundamental recipe for happiness, "Set your heart upon God, and not upon things, upon Cause and not upon manifestation, upon Principle and not upon form." As the old landmarks disappear one by one beneath the rising tide of the new life, we shall go boldly on, knowing that the best is yet to be, and that "Eye hath not seen, nor ear heard, neither hath it entered into the heart of man the things that God hath prepared for them that love Him," and put Him first.

Each of these Ages or ways of knowing God has a dominant quality or character of its own which distinguishes it from the other eleven. Just as each nation has an indefinable quality which all its natives possess in common, no matter how much they may otherwise differ among themselves, and which marks them off from all other groups of people; just as each of the great religions has its own special character or atmosphere that arises from the particular aspects of Universal Truth upon which it lays stress, so each Age has its own peculiar character arising from the particular aspects of Truth with which it deals. The quality which distinguishes the new Aquarian Age—so distinct in every respect from the late Piscean Age—is called for convenience "Uranus," and in a general way all the activities and expressions of the Aquarian Age will be Uranian. Now this is interesting because it gives us a broad idea of the sort of thing that we may expect. Uranus is usually spoken of as a disrupter or smasher, but it must be remembered that this does not necessarily, as is too often assumed, imply real destruction. It is well that the less good should be destroyed if this means that the better is given an opportunity of taking its place. Those who understand the Truth of Being are well aware that what we call death and destruction are usually but the prelude to something better and finer. What is the death of Monday but the birth of Tuesday, the death of the old year but the birth of the new one, the pulling down of an old house but the prelude to the building of a newer and better one. And so the New Age, while at first it may seem to be destructive, will, in fact, be destructive only of ideas which, while good and necessary in their own time, have now been outgrown by humanity, and could only remain as a hindrance.

Consider the state of mind of the chick at the moment when he has become fully formed and ready for a free and independent life; but just before the shell has broken. How delightfully comfortable the inside of that shell feels. How warm, how snug, how safe. How terrifying to a nervous chick must be the prospect of being thrown out into a wide, cold, unknown, seemingly infinite world. Yet, because he is now mature and ready for the great adventure, the warm shell which has been so necessary and so comforting to him up to that moment, would, if he attempted to remain in it, very soon smother and destroy him. He has outgrown that phase, and out he must go, willing or not. A brave chick, on the contrary, one who has faith in the essential goodness of life, and the innate friendliness of things, goes out into the new world conquering and to conquer. Here Uranus comes as a smasher indeed but it is as the smasher of a prison, and the liberator of a captive soul.

Humanity is now very much in the position of the chick who has outgrown his old environment, and must boldly step out into something new and strange and grand.

Uranus is also spoken of as a symbol of democracy and freedom, and at other times it is referred to as standing for autocracy; and this seeming contradiction has puzzled many; but the actual truth is that Uranus stands neither for democracy nor autocracy as such, but for *individuality*. Now the free expression of individuality must mean true democracy in the sense that every human soul shall have an equal opportunity for true self-expression as the thing that God intended it to be, and, on the other hand, as the master of its own fate and the captain of its own soul, it becomes the autocrat of its own life, answerable to God alone and unrestricted in its development by any tyrannical outside interference. That is Uranus.

We have actually been in the Aquarian Age for a number of years already, but it is only now that we are beginning to feel the full effects of the change. Nature knows nothing of sudden jerky transitions. With her all is gradual, and so each New Age steals slowly upon the human consciousness, and more than one generation goes by before the changes become easily observable. We must remember that in a period lasting about twenty-one hundred and fifty years, half a century or a century does not mean so much as one might suppose at first sight. Today the introductory period technically known as the "cusp" is over, and we are now in the full tide of Aquarian life. As we look about us in the world we are at once struck by the number of Aquarian manifestations everywhere in being. The new inventions, for instance, that have transformed the world since the childhood of middle aged people, are nearly all Aquarian-Uranian in character. Electricity, which in its various forms, as electric light and traction, the telegraph and the telephone, and now the radio, has done so much to make the new world different from the old one —electricity is essentially Uranian. Every application of electricity, for instance, is the individualization at a particular point of manifestation— lamp, motor, bell, microphone, and so forth—of a general current. And everyone who has experimented however slightly, with an electric current knows that when wrongly handled it is exceedingly sudden and violent in its reactions—a disrupter or wrecker. Yet, when employed constructively and intelligently, it does more than any other material thing to liberate the human soul from the fetters of drudgery and physical limitations. The telephone abolishes distance and is man's first partial demonstration over the space limitation. The electric light indoors and out-of-doors has been the finger of God in promoting education. cleanliness, sanitation, and all other good things that wither in darkness and flourish in light. Electric traction, when it is given a fair chance, will empty our city slums and restore our people to God's countryside. The radio is rapidly breaking down many of the artificial barriers that formerly divided man from man. Within each nation it is destroying social prejudices right and left by giving a correct standard of speech to all classes, and already the change wrought by this is quite noticeable. Internationally the radio laughs at frontiers, and, thanks to its efforts, it will no longer be possible, however much reactionary authorities may desire it, to isolate any body of human beings from the common stock of human knowledge and human progress. The Inquisition would have been powerless against the radio broadcast and a receiving set in every home.

Next to electricity the internal combustion engine in the form of the automobile and the airplane has probably done most to change the face of the world, and this too is essentially Uranian-Aquarian. Consider how fundamentally individual a thing an automobile is, as compared say with the railroad train. Indeed, one could hardly get a more complete expression of the distinction between mass compulsion and free individuality than in considering the difference between taking a prescribed journey to a prescribed time-table in a train and the untrammeled exploring of the countryside in a car. Internationally the airplane has simply abolished military frontiers. Military authors are still writing in terms of strategic frontiers, but statesmen know to their secret consternation that they are gone.

The Aquarian Age, in fact, is to be the age of personal freedom. It is no mere coincidence that its arrival marks the emancipation of women as a sex, and that in the present age the children too have at last been conceded rights as individuals, and are no longer regarded simply as the personal property of their parents.

We have seen that what are called the Twelve Signs of the Zodiac really signify twelve different ways of knowing God. Most thinking people have already given up the old childish way of thinking of God as just a big superior kind of man, and as the Aquarian Age advances the great bulk of mankind will gradually outgrow that limitation too. The truth is that actually God is All in All: Infinite Mind, Life, Truth, and Love. God is Infinite Intelligence, Unfathomable Wisdom, Unspeakable Beauty. In repeating these words, we get, of course, a hopelessly inadequate realization of what they must really mean, and the true nature of God in its fullness is so immense and wonderful and undreamed of by us, that in practice it takes the human race not thousands, but millions of years to reach its full comprehension. Even to grasp the fact that God is Incorporeal Mind, perfect Principle, has taken us literally hundreds of thousands of years; and we shall not all reach even this point for some time to come yet. And when we have grasped that stupendous reality, the Truth about God still opens out in front of us to Infinity.

Just as each Age is a special lesson that humanity has to learn about God, so in each Age there is a special outstanding teacher who teaches the lesson of that Age, and demonstrates it in a complete and unmistakable manner. The great Race Teacher of the Age of Aries was Abraham. Abraham raised the standard of the One God, perfect, not made with hands, eternal in the heavens. Abraham when he received his enlightenment came straight out from idolatry and, forestalling Moses, said, in effect—Know, Oh Israel the Lord thy God is One God—Thou shalt have no other gods before Him—Thou shalt not make unto thyself graven images.

How tremendous a step forward this was in the history of humanity, can only be appreciated by those who have investigated the old civilizations, with their welter of competing gods, and their futile, grotesque, and sometimes obscene idolatries. An old tradition tells that the immediate family of Abram (as he then was) were actually manufacturers and sellers of idols, and so, in coming out for the One purely Spiritual God, he was obliged to break with his own immediate people. It may well have been so, for is it not the maker of images who is most likely, given an honest heart, to become the iconoclast.

Abraham, having launched the new Age, that of Aries or the Ram, passed into history, and his work went on with the usual ebb and flow characteristic of human activity. Now it should be noted that that Age is called symbolically the Age of the Ram or Sheep, and that all through the Bible sheep are used to symbolize thoughts, and that the great outstanding lesson of the Bible is that we have to watch our thoughts, because whatever we think with conviction will come to us sooner or later. It is important to note in this connection how many of the great saints and heroes of the Bible were at one time shepherds. Jacob, Moses, David, Cyrus the Mede ("His Anointed"), and many of lesser importance all served an apprenticeship in the keeping of sheep—the right control of thought. And of the many titles that have been given to our Lord himself, he would probably have preferred that of the Good Shepherd. Did he not say, "The Good Shepherd gives his life for his sheep." In all this we see the influence of the Ariean lesson working itself out in the race thought. Egypt, in the Bible, stands for materialism, sin, sickness, and death ("Out of Egypt have I called my son") and very significantly we are told that the Egyptians harbored an undying enmity and hatred for a shepherd. All this, of course, is not to be taken literally as a reflection upon the people who lived in the Nile valley, and were no worse, if no better, than other men, but as a symbolical description of the working out of natural laws. It is an interesting fact that right down to the present day in the Jewish synagogues where the Ariean Age still lingers, the Ram's horn remains as a living symbol.

The Age which followed the Ariean Age, and from

which we have recently emerged, and which might well be called the epoch of orthodox Christianity, is known as the Age of Pisces or the Fishes. The great leader and prophet of that Age was, of course, Jesus Christ, and we know that in the early days of Christianity he was symbolized among his followers as a fish. The cross, the great emblem of Christianity in later times, was not used in the first days. People were then a little ashamed to think of the Master in connection with a Roman gibbet. In the catacombs of Rome and elsewhere we find inscriptions of the early Christians in which Jesus is referred to as the fish. This had the further advantage of throwing their persecutors off the scent. Actually, the cross as a symbol of physical matter and physical limitation, is far, far older than Christianity; but that is by the way. Suffice it to say that the Age of Pisces was constantly being announced in symbols by all sorts of people, many of whom realized not at all what it was that they were doing. The great mediaeval church, for instance, centered her authority, for practical purposes, in the bishop, and the distinguishing symbol of a bishop is, of course, the mitre. And what is the mitre but a fish's head worn as a headdress. Jesus said, "I will make you fishers of men," and actually his first disciples were fishermen, just as the Old Testament leaders were shepherds.

THE ZODIAC AND THE BIBLE

All through the Bible, and throughout the old occult tradition in general, the fish stands as a symbol of wisdom, and wisdom is then understood as the technical term for the knowledge of the Allness of God and of the power of prayer. Notice that the fish lives in the depths of the waters (the human soul) from which it has to be, so to say, fished out, and it is silent and non-assertive. It has to be sought with patience and gentleness. It is not to be hunted down violently like a wolf.

The Aquarian Age is the age of the Man with the Water Pot ("Seek ye a man bearing a pot of water")—and who is the man with the water pot? Why, the gardener, of course, and so the interpretative symbol of the New Age is to be the Gardener. Man having graduated as a Shepherd, and as a Fisherman, now becomes a Gardener, and this title nicely expresses the kind of work that he has to do in his new rôle. We have now reached the stage when the lesson of the need for thought control having been learned, and the *Santa Sophia* or Holy Wisdom having been contacted and appreciated, the two things must be united mentally in our everyday practice.

Modern science is making some of its greatest strides in the realm of psychology, so that indeed psychology may today be called the handmaid of metaphysics, and psychology is insisting more and more that the conscious and the subconscious minds stand almost exactly in the relationship of gardener and garden. The gardener sows his seed in the soil that he has prepared; he waters the ground and, as far as possible, he selects a site upon which the sun will shine; but he does not try to make the seed grow. He leaves that to Nature. So, in spiritual treatment or scientific prayer, we speak the Word, but we leave it to the Divine Power to make the demonstration. "I have planted; Apollos watered; but God gave the increase." The dominant note of the New Age is to be Spiritual development and Spiritual demonstration.

At this stage the question naturally presents itself—Who is, or who is to be, the great teacher and prophet of our new Aquarian Age. Well, it seems that there is no lack of candidates for the position. All over the world sundry people are laying claim to this high office, or their followers are claiming it for them. No time need be wasted over this sort of thing. Did not the Master warn us that false Christs would arise who would deceive, if it were possible, the very elect.

The wonderful fact is that now, after all these thousands and thousands of years of upward striving, we have at last reached the stage where humanity is ready to do without personal prophets of any kind, and to contact the Living God at first hand for itself. Never until now has this been possible for the mass of the people. Individuals from time to time have reached this stage, but never until now has it been possible for the great majority. Always they have had to have some concrete symbol. First of all, a coarse and palpable idol such as was denounced by Abraham and Moses, and afterwards by Mohammed. Later when they had passed beyond that stage, they still demanded a man to worship, or even a book, something tangible and concrete to lay hold of mentally. But now, chiefly owing to the work that Jesus did in the race mind nineteen hundred years ago, it has become possible for all men and women, if they will, to grasp the idea of the Impersonal Christ Truth; to grasp the truth that their own Indwelling Christ—the Inner Light of the Quakers—is always with them to inspire, to heal, to strengthen and comfort, and illumine. Jesus said, unless I go away the Holy Spirit cannot come, meaning that as long as he was with them they would cling to his personality instead of finding the Infinite, Incorporeal God for themselves; and this is very largely what the orthodox churches have always done.

And so the Great World Teacher of the new age is not to be any man or woman, or any textbook, or any organization, but the Indwelling Christ, that each individual is to find and contact for himself There is a simple test by which anyone can tell a true teacher from a false one. It is this: If he points you to his own personality; if he makes special claims for himself; if he says that he has received any special privileges from God that are not equally accessible to the whole human race anywhere; if he attempts in his own name or in that of an organization to establish under any pretense a monopoly of the truth about God, then, however imposing his credentials, however pleasing his personality may be, he is a false teacher, and you had better have nothing to do with him. If, on the contrary, he tells you to look away from himself, to seek the Presence of God in your own heart, and to use books, lectures, and churches only as a means to that one end, then, however humble his efforts may be, however lacking his own demonstration may seem, he is nevertheless a true teacher and is giving you the Bread of Life.

It takes humanity about twenty-six thousand years to go through this class of twelve lessons about God, which we call the Zodiac. But of course, we have been through that class many times already—remember that the race is far older than most people think—and we shall have to go through it many times more, but each time we go through the same lessons at a much higher level, garnering a different *quality* of knowledge, for it is not an endless circle, but an upward reaching spiral.

Now this change through which the world is going at the present time, which is covering the front pages of the newspapers with sensations, and filling the hearts of men with fear and misgivings, this change, as it happens, is much more than the mere passing from one Sign or Age to another, such as happened in passing from Aries into Pisces, from Taurus into Aries, from Gemini into Taurus, and so on. Actually our present change is the greatest that the human race has made for about fifty-two thousand years. That is to say, we have been twice around the Zodiac since we last made such a giant step forward as the present one. Not since the mass of humanity became capable of using the abstract mind (it is quite true that precious few of them ever use it now, but they all could if they wanted to and were trained for it) has it gained such an increase in Power. It is now possible for everyone if he so wishes to contact the Spiritual Power which lies all around us, which is God, always ready at a moment's notice to help us in any way we may need.

This means that while the race as a whole moves forward relatively slowly on the path of spiritual development, *there is now no reason at all why any individual who really desires it should not cut out all intermediate steps and make the Great Demonstration at his own pace, irrespective of any material circumstances of time, or Zodiac, or anything else whatever.* The qualities he will need for success are a single-minded pursuit of Truth and the whole-hearted practice of the highest that he knows at the moment.

So now we see that the Zodiac is really one of the great cosmic symbols, perhaps the greatest of them all, a diagram of the unfoldment of the human soul, and not the mere physical fact of the Precession of the Equinoxes. Not just a kind of circular railroad track for fortune-telling, but one of the deepest mysteries of the soul.

The question of *when* the great changes herein referred to will take place is naturally one that does not admit of a precise answer. It may, however, be said with confidence that what will appear to us as the most revolutionary and far-reaching upheavals in the circumstances of human life will be all over and done with in from twenty to twenty-five years from now; and that some very striking and important changes are already under way and will become perhaps startlingly apparent within the next few years.

These changes will hardly go through without a certain amount of disturbance and temporary chaos, as we have seen; but we know that Man as a race will emerge with flying colors, purified, strengthened, and emancipated. But what of the individual? Well, individuals may have a bad time in certain cases, but your personal fate will depend upon one thing, and one thing only—the condition in which you keep your consciousness. If you maintain an attitude of mental peace and good-will towards all; if you really root out of your own heart every atom of hostility and condemnation for your brother man, no matter who he may be, then you will be safe. As Jesus promised: "Nothing shall by any means hurt you." You will pass through the hottest fires unmoved and unscathed. But, if you allow yourself to be drawn, if only by mental acquiescence, into any current of hatred against anybody, against any nation, or any race, or any class or any religious sect, or any other person or body of people, under any pretense whatsoever; then you will have forfeited your protection and you will have to take the consequences. If you allow yourself to be carried away by any political, religious, or newspaper campaign of hatred, no matter how self-righteously it may be camouflaging itself, then you will be laying yourself open to any destructive tendencies that may be going. It is for you to choose, knowing that as you do choose, so it will be done unto you.

Of course, the only real protection in any kind of danger is the knowledge of scientific prayer, or the Practice of the Presence of God; and so have not we who understand this Truth and how to apply it in practice, a sacred duty and responsibility to do all that lies in our power to spread that knowledge now as widely and as quickly as possible.

The Secret Place

THE Ninety-first Psalm is one of the very greatest chapters in the whole Bible. It is one of those chapters that everybody knows by heart. Yet, like so many familiar Bible passages, it is unfortunately among the least understood. It must, of course, be interpreted in the spiritual way, and it is only thus that the true meaning is arrived at. Like the rest of Scripture, the underlying thought is developed through a series of symbols, and it is by the appreciation of the values lying behind these that the power of this prayer is appropriated.

The Book of Psalms has been called "The Little Bible," and it certainly forms a matchless treasure-house of spiritual riches. This wonderful collection of poems, lyrical, dramatic, elegiac, contains something to fit every mood, and to meet every need of humanity. All through the centuries of both Old Testament and

Christian history, they have been a never failing source of inspiration and comfort for men and women of every kind and every walk of life, and it is safe to say that no soul in need has ever turned to the Book of Psalms in vain.

The Ninety-first Psalm when scientifically understood, is found to be one of the most powerful prayers ever written. All sorts of people have got themselves out of every conceivable kind of trouble by working on this prayer every day, in the spiritual way. Other cases are on record of people who had not prayed for years turning to this prayer in some great emergency and overcoming their difficulty; with only the surface meaning to help them. It will easily be seen, therefore, how well worthwhile it is to make oneself thoroughly acquainted with at least the principal ideas contained within it, for then one has always ready to hand a practical prayer of unparalleled power.

The best way to get the most out of this psalm is to read it through quietly; pause

THE SECRET PLACE

after each clause to consider the meaning as given in the commentary; assent to this mentally; and then pass on to the next. Remember that all this is praying. Prayer is, essentially, thinking about God—not necessarily addressing God, helpful though this may be at times—and while you are working on this psalm, analyzing the text, and considering the meaning in your own mind, you are praying, and in a very efficient way too. If you are in a specific difficulty, and particularly if you are rather fearful, you will find, after working through the prayer once or twice or perhaps three times, that most of your fear will have gone, and that you are now looking at things from a different point of view—and this is the change in mentality that brings about results.

Let us then consider the prayer in detail, taking it verse by verse.

He that dwelleth in the secret place of the most High shall abide under the shadow of the Almighty. The Secret Place of the Most High is your own consciousness.

and this fact is the most important practical discovery in the whole science of religion. The error that is usually made is to suppose the Secret Place of the Most High to be somewhere outside of yourself; across the sea, or up in the sky probably. This error is usually fatal to our hopes, because our prospects of success in prayer depend upon our succeeding in getting some degree of contact with God, and since He is only to be contacted within, and never without, as long as we are looking without we must naturally fail in our objective. Jesus emphasized this truth again and again; indeed it is the foundation-stone of his whole teaching. "Seek first the Kingdom of God," he said, and, when asked where that kingdom could be found, replied, "The Kingdom of God is within you." And again he said that when we pray we are to enter into the closet and shut the door, meaning, to retire in thought within our own consciousness and to withdraw our attention from outer things. In fact, this doctrine of the Secret Place and the wonders that can happen therein is taught right throughout the Bible.

To abide under the shadow of the Almighty means to live under the protection of God Himself. "Under the shadow," is a dramatic, oriental expression for safety. Eastern people, and especially those with a desert background, such as the people of Palestine, look upon the sun as a danger, even an enemy, from which they need to be safeguarded. In the West, as a rule, we look upon him as our greatest friend, and we can hardly get enough sun to satisfy us; but in the East it is otherwise. There, shade is sanctuary, or safety—"the shadow of a great rock in a weary land." The exhausted traveller, on attaining his goal, sinks down in the shade for his long sought rest, feeling that now at last he is safe.

Let us note that here God is called "The Almighty," this title being selected from among the many other titles that the Bible has for God, in order to impress us at this point with the fact that He really is Almighty, and that He can therefore overcome our present difficulty for us, no matter how big it may seem at the moment—"With God all things are possible." Consider, however, that the promise is made to "him that *dwelleth.*" If we only run into the Secret Place now and again when we are in trouble, we can scarcely be said to dwell there. God will always come to our rescue *whenever* we pray, but if we seldom think of Him at other times, we may experience considerable difficulty in making our contact in an emergency; or we may even be so perturbed as to forget altogether to pray. By means of regular daily prayer and meditation we dwell in the Secret Place, and then we may expect to abide under the shadow, and to enjoy the protection of the Power that is indeed All Powerful.

At this point we notice a change in the form of the psalm from the third person to the first. This is a literary stroke of rare skill. Observe that the poem opens by definitely announcing the irresistible power of prayer. It states a general Cosmic Law in a form of scientific detachment. In order to bring home to you with unmistakable clearness the fact that this law applies to you, as much as to anything or anyone in the universe, and that by no possibility could you be an exception, it now changes over to the first person and makes you say "I." In the language of metaphysics, it compels you to voice the I AM.

I will say of the Lord, He is my refuge and my fortress: my God; in Him will I trust. The Lord means God, in particular your own knowledge of Truth, as that knowledge is in itself the Presence of God in the one who knows it, his Indwelling Christ. How can knowledge be a presence? Secular knowledge, which is intellectual, cannot; but the true knowledge of God is not an intellectual theory; it is an actual experience—not a thing of the head, but of the heart—and this is indeed a Presence. It is indeed one's own higher, or Real Self. It is pure Spirit. It is at one with God. As a general rule, people contact this Real Self only vaguely and occasionally at first, often calling the experience "intuition." Then, if they pray regularly in the scientific way, and especially if they frequently pray for inspiration, the flickering gleams of intuition gradually magnify and strengthen into a clear and definite sense of the Presence of God, when He really becomes their Lord. The student should understand, however, that it is by no means necessary to get this clear sense of the Divine Presence in order to have the help of God. The very fact that you are praying at all means that the action of God is taking place in your consciousness, and the action of God must have results.

In Him will I trust. However worried or depressed you may be, however full of doubts and misgivings, still the very fact that you are praying means that you have at least enough faith for that. The faith to go on praying in the midst of doubts about results is the tiny grain of mustard seed that Jesus says is sufficient for practical purposes. "In Him will I trust" is an expression of your determination to trust in God in spite of appearances. It means that you have now determined to trust practically in God by ceasing to worry and fear. This is the legitimate and spiritual use of the will. Your will is a Divine faculty, and has its own place in the spiritual life. Of course, the will can be misused. We must not try to bring events to pass by the direct exertion of will power, even to produce a bodily healing; but the will must be employed to say whether we are going to pray or not to pray; whether we are going to give way to fear or to refuse to do so; whether we are going to yield to temptation or not. In the case of temptation, it is notorious how often will power fails, but that is because the will should be employed, not to fight the temptation directly, but to choose to pray about it instead of giving way to it.

This phrase means, not that you have already attained a sense of security, but that —though you still feel yourself to be in **danger**—you are choosing by the **correct** exercise of your power of will to put your trust in the Love of God, instead of in the impending danger.

At this point the poem dramatically changes again, this time from the first person to the second. You have now voiced the I AM; you have recognized both the power and the goodness of God; and the fact of the living Presence of God in you and with you. You have determined, by a spiritual act of will, to trust in God, and by this procedure you have brought the action of God into play in your life. You have done your part. Now the Word of Truth is represented as addressing you with an authoritative assurance that your prayer will be answered, that in some way or other—not by any means necessarily in the way that you expect, but in some good way—you will be rescued from your difficulty. Again the Eastern instinct for dramatic form drives the great truth home with unequalled power in this employment of the second person.

THE SECRET PLACE

Surely He shall deliver thee from the snare of the fowler, and from the noisome pestilence. He shall cover thee with His feathers, and under His wings shalt thou trust: His truth shall be thy shield and buckler. Needless to say, both the fowler's snare and the noisome pestilence are to be interpreted in the most general sense as including any kind of danger, material, moral, or spiritual, that can threaten your welfare; and very apt descriptions they are of many of the perils that beset the children of men in their daily round. You are, however, to have no apprehension, for your protection is now assured to you in one of those beautiful illustrations from simple everyday life in which the Bible abounds. What child has not watched with delight the familiar farmyard scene in which the motherly old hen, at the slightest threat of danger, gathers the little chicks under her wings, covering them "with her feathers," from any possible harm. Thus does God shield you from all danger once you have elected to trust

Him. *His truth shall be thy shield and buckler.* It is the knowledge of the Truth about God and man that makes the demonstration. One does not *do* something with Divine Truth; it is the knowing of that Truth that in itself heals the condition. *Ye shall know the truth, and the truth shall make you free.*

Thou shalt not be afraid for the terror by night; nor for the arrow that flieth by day; Nor for the pestilence that walketh in darkness; nor for the destruction that wasteth at noonday. These two verses together with verse 13, lower down, constitute a superb analysis of the rationale of man's psychological nature. The respective characteristics of our conscious and subconscious minds are contrasted with unsurpassed insight. For practical purposes, all our troubles may be classified as belonging to either the conscious or the subconscious mind, and have to be dealt with accordingly. The arrow that flieth by day and the destruction that wasteth at noon refer to any difficulty of which

THE SECRET PLACE

you are consciously aware, whether that difficulty be a physical ailment, a business problem, trouble with another person, or what-not. The point here is that you are aware of the difficulty, and that you are seeking in one way or another to overcome it. It is, so to say, a daytime problem.

The terror by night and the pestilence that walketh in darkness, on the contrary, imply something that, unknown to you, is working in your subconscious mind, or, unsuspected by you in the world outside of yourself. Modern psychology has shown conclusively that most of our difficulties have their roots far out of sight in the depths of the subconscious, and that these subconscious minds, in fact, contain an enormous amount of material whose presence we little suspect. These are indeed terrors of the mental night and pestilences of the darkness. In a less personal sense, they refer to any danger from outside of yourself of which you may be unaware. An impending accident, for instance, would come under this heading, or any hostile activities by people secretly inimical to you. If, let us say, an enemy were covertly working against you, or, as occasionally happens, a business partner or an employee were acting to your detriment, unsuspected by you, such things would come under this heading of hidden trouble.

A thousand shall fall at thy side, and ten thousand at thy right hand; but it shall not come nigh thee. Only with thine eyes shalt thou behold and see the reward of the wicked. This clause has been gravely misunderstood. It has been taken to indicate some kind of favoritism on the part of God, whereas, of course, such a thing is utterly impossible. "No respecter of persons." It really means, quite simply, that prayer does change things, that those who pray are saved from trouble that would otherwise overtake them, and that does, in fact, overtake those who do not pray. The word "wicked" originally meant bewitched, and the wicked need not necessarily be conscious wrong-doers, but are much more frequently just those who do not rely upon God, or trouble to say their prayers, because they are bewitched or deceived by materialism, or atheism, or by simple doubt in the efficacy of prayer. Because they do not pray they cannot expect to escape from trouble and do not succeed in doing so.

Because thou hast made the Lord, which is my refuge, even the most High, thy habitation; There shall no evil befall thee, neither shall any plague come nigh thy dwelling. This is one of the most definite and concrete promises given in the whole Bible. In all the many declarations of the nearness and certainty of God's help, which abound in the Scriptures, not one is more precise or more definite than this. It says that once you have made this Divine Christ Power your refuge, by living regularly in the spiritual consciousness—making it your habitation—no trouble can touch you. Could the thing possibly be more pointedly and convincingly stated?

The Bible has an idiom that is all its own, and in this idiom the word "promise" is the name given to a statement of some metaphysical law. It is not used in the sense in which you promise a person to do something at some future date, meaning an agreement or pledge. Such a promise is supposed to be a matter of choice on the part of its author who says in effect, "I am willing to do such a thing next week or next year. I choose now to agree to do it." Thus one may promise to pay a sum of money in six months' time, or one may promise a child to take it to a show next week. A Bible "promise" is a statement of a natural law in metaphysics, just as a "law" of physics such as Boyle's law or Ohm's law is a statement of the consequences, upon the physical plane, that will naturally follow upon certain other occurrences.

So, a "Bible promise" is a statement of the consequences that naturally follow from certain thoughts and states of consciousness. If Boyle's law were written in the Bible idiom, it would read something like this: "As I live, saith the Lord, whenever thou shalt double the pressure of a gas, thou shalt halve the volume, temperature remaining constant." In the language of natural science, our Bible promise would run: "By meditating regularly on the Presence of God with you, and directing your life in accordance with that fact, you become immune from any kind of danger."

For He shall give His angels charge over thee, to keep thee in all thy ways. They shall bear thee up in their hands, lest thou dash thy foot against a stone. This is one of the very loveliest of all the promises in the Bible. For tender beauty it stands alone. Re-read it carefully now, and ask yourself whether human language could possibly say anything more exquisite than this, or promise anything more wonderful. *He shall give His angels charge over thee to keep thee in all thy ways*—and it is meant for you and for me. It might have seemed appropriate enough that some extraordinary or exalted Being should be given an escort of angels, as a bodyguard, to surround him, to support him, to keep him in all his ways. But the Bible is the book of Everyman, and this promise is given to you and to me.

It would be no bad thing if you made this single verse the subject of careful meditation every day for a month. If, in that way, you came to realize, however feebly, the real significance of this promise—that you are to be in the charge of angels and safeguarded in all your ways (not merely in certain ways, but in all your ways), safeguarded for bodily health, for food, clothing, rent, and the other necessaries of life; for right activity and self-expression; for congenial companionship; safeguarded from temptation and from fear as well—what a staggering difference this would make in your life.

Thou shalt tread upon the lion and adder; the young lion and the dragon shalt thou trample under feet. Having sung of the invincible protection and loving kindness of God in this glorious burst of poetry, the inspired writer now re-states the same idea from the scientific or psychological point of view. The great Illumined Ones who wrote the Bible under Divine inspiration well knew all the teaching of modern psychology. They understood human nature as no other teachers have ever understood it, and they wrote of it in their own way as no others have ever written of it before or since. The ideas concerning the subconscious mind and the part it plays in our scheme of things, which have lately been put forward by investigators like Freud and Jung and others, novel though they appear to the modern world, were all quite familiar to the great Initiates of the Bible—that is to say, the portions of these teachings which are correct for, of course, they are on many points at variance with fact. Moses, Isaiah, John, and the author of this psalm, for example, knew all that is to be known about the subconscious mind and the way in which it functions. They knew all about what we call complexes and neuroses, the unconscious motive, the phenomena of dissociation and splitting, and many other things too that our psychologists have not yet discovered. Here the psalmist draws a further contrast between the subconscious danger and the consciously realized difficulty, as a development of verses 5 and 6. Now it is the adder and the dragon put against the lion. The lion stands for a difficulty about which we are informed, particularly now a great or intimidating difficulty, one of which we are so afraid that it seems to us a very lion in our path. The lion has his faults; he is indeed extraordinarily undesirable as a companion —ferocious, pitiless, quick as lightning, strong as steel; but credit he must be given for one major virtue—he is no sneak. He rushes at you in the open; you know what you have to meet; and can take your measures. How different, on the other hand, is the attack of the adder, or snake; for it is hidden. It creeps upon you in the dark, and ordinarily you have no sense of danger until the blow falls. You cannot fight this enemy squarely, because you cannot see it. Here, of course, we again recognize subconscious trouble, and in the repeated and parallel phrase so characteristic of Hebrew poetry the lion becomes a young or particularly vigorous lion, and the adder becomes a dragon, and this is the Bible term for what in modern psychology is called a complex. A complex is a group of ideas heavily charged with emotion and hidden away in the subconscious mind. These emotions usually have their roots in one of the great primary instincts of human nature, and this fact endows them with what is often a terribly destructive power.

And here you are promised that your complexes shall be dissolved by the Christ Truth, the realization of God. Utterly dissolved. Completely dispersed. *Trampled under feet,* is the telling phrase employed to express their complete annihilation. There is nothing that can be done by psycho-analysis or any other form of psycho-therapy that cannot be much better **done by scientific prayer, or the Practice** of the Presence of God. Prayer, which is the appeal to God, as distinct from any form of mere mental treatment, goes straight to the seat of the trouble, wherever it may be, without need of any direction on your part. When you pray about any specific difficulty, enough prayer will remove that difficulty by removing its real mental cause, whatever or wherever it may be, even though you do not in the least suspect the cause, or even though you may be erroneously attributing it to quite a wrong cause. However deep down or far back in the subconscious life the trouble may be, the Christ Truth will find it and redeem it. *He descended into hell.*

The last three verses constitute the final stanza. They are in themselves a glorious psalm of ringing joy and triumph. Even when used alone, they form a complete and wonderful spiritual treatment. Here once more we find a dramatic change in the presentation, the prayer being again thrown into the first person, again with the object of compelling you to voice the

I AM on the highest note. Thus your simple prayer gradually develops into nothing less than the Logos, the creative Word of God, spoken through you, which goes forth conquering and to conquer, and shall by no means return void.

Because he hath set his love upon me, therefore I will deliver him. This is one of those gnomic sayings in which the Bible abounds, where an ocean of teaching is crystallized into a phrase. It is a definite statement that you are to be delivered from your difficulty because you have set your love upon God. That; definitely and simply. There is nothing hypothetical or contingent here; no conditions whatever either expressed or implied. The statement indicates the accomplished fact—the fixed decision, as it were—*I will deliver him.* And why?—*because he hath set his love upon me.* "But, alas," you may say, "this cannot apply to me, because, to be honest, I do not really feel any very strong sense of love for God. How I should like to!—but I do not." To which the answer is, that your love for God is not an emotion. It has really nothing to do with the feelings at all. In these matters emotion is too often misleading. We demonstrate and prove our love for God by saying our prayers, and by refusing to recognize error as having any power over us; by declining, out of loyalty to God, to accept anything less than the perfect harmony which is His Will. *If you love Me, keep My commandments.* By the very fact that you have been praying about a difficulty, going through this psalm, for instance, you have been setting your love upon God, no matter how depressed or how doubtful you may have felt. And because you have set your love upon Him, He will deliver you.

I will set him on high because he hath known My Name. In the Bible the "name" of anything means the nature or character of that thing. Now the nature of God is perfect, omnipresent, all-powerful good, boundless love; and to "know" this is to be set on high above all your difficulties— that is, to be taken out of them, into freedom, security and happiness. This is because, in Biblical language, to know a thing is not a mere intellectual apprehension, but involves a certain degree of understanding and realization. So we see that when we have, through our prayers, attained some real appreciation of the Allness of God, our troubles disappear.

The last two verses gather up, so to say, all the implications and promises of this most wonderful stanza, and present them to the fearful or doubting heart as a song of triumph; promising counsel, and guidance in perplexity, salvation in trouble, and a long and joyous career, culminating in complete spiritual triumph. *He shall call upon me, and I will answer him: I will be with him in trouble; I will deliver him, and honor him. With long life will I satisfy him, and show him my salvation.*

LIGHT AND SALVATION

1. The Lord is my light and my salvation; whom shall I fear? the Lord is the strength of my life; of whom shall I be afraid?

2. When the wicked, even mine enemies and my foes, came upon me to eat up my flesh, they stumbled and fell.

3. Though an host should encamp against me, my heart shall not fear: though war should rise against me, in this will I be confident.

4. One thing have I desired of the Lord, that will I seek after; that I may dwell in the house of the Lord all the days of my life, to behold the beauty of the Lord, and to enquire in his temple.

5. For in the time of trouble he shall hide me in his pavilion: in the secret of his tabernacle shall he hide me; he shall set me up upon a rock.

6. And now shall mine head be lifted up above mine enemies round about me: therefore will I offer in his tabernacle sacrifices of joy; I will sing, yea, I will sing praises unto the Lord.

7. Hear, O Lord, when I cry with my voice: have mercy also upon me, and answer me.

8. When thou saidst, Seek ye my face; my heart said unto thee, Thy face, Lord, will I seek.

9. Hide not thy face far from me; put not thy servant away in anger: thou hast been my help; leave me not, neither forsake me, O God of my salvation.

LIGHT AND SALVATION

10. When my father and my mother forsake me, then the Lord will take me up.

11. Teach me thy way, O Lord, and lead me in a plain path, because of mine enemies.

12. Deliver me not over unto the will of mine enemies: for false witnesses are risen up against me, and such as breathe out cruelty.

13. I had fainted, unless I had believed to see the goodness of the Lord in the land of the living.

14. Wait upon the Lord; be of good courage, and he shall strengthen thine heart: wait, I say, on the Lord.

THE 27TH PSALM

Light and Salvation

NE of the quickest ways of getting out of trouble is to use this Psalm intelligently. The Twenty-seventh Psalm is one of the great treatments or meditations in the Bible. Treatment is a convenient technical term we use for scientific prayer, which is directed to the overcoming of a specific difficulty. When trouble of any kind comes into one's life it is because he has allowed his consciousness to fall to the level where fear and limitation can reach him. A treatment consists in working on one's consciousness to raise it to the spiritual level where the trouble, whatever it is, disappears. Any mental activity which enables us thus to raise the spiritual standard of the soul is a form of prayer, and the Bible abounds in such forms.

The history of a problem or a difficulty is often this: The student is worried about something, or he feels ill. As soon as he

LIGHT AND SALVATION

realizes what has happened he, owing to his knowledge of Truth, declines to accept the condition at its face value in the way that most people do; and he proceeds, in one way or another, perhaps with the help of a prayer such as this, to bring about the necessary raising of his thought. He reads the Psalm carefully, interprets it spiritually, allows his mind to dwell upon the principles enunciated, appropriates them to himself, and repudiates the negative suggestion, whatever it was, thus regaining his peace of mind. And when this has been accomplished the trouble is found to disappear.

The Lord is my light and my salvation; whom shall I fear? the Lord is the strength of my life; of whom shall I be afraid?

This one verse is a perfect little treatment in itself; indeed it is one of the most complete texts in the whole Bible. It is a text that might well be written up over the portals of every church and every school in the land, for within it is contained in embryo the complete Jesus Christ message. Consider what it says. It postulates not merely the existence of God, but the living Presence of God in man, for the Lord here means your own Indwelling Christ, the I Am. Then it goes on to state that God in you, the Inner Light, is no mere passive or static presence, but a dynamic power to do everything for you that you can possibly need to have done. Just consider what this one phrase promises—light, salvation, and strength.

You will find that these three words cover very completely everything that man needs, for they really mean understanding, power, and demonstration—and what more can you want than that?

To begin with light. "There is no darkness but ignorance," and in the last analysis all human weaknesses and tribulations are really but a lack of the Divine Light. "Light, more light," said the dying Goethe, and that has been the intuitive cry of humanity through all its history. But God is Light, the Bible tells us, and in Him is no darkness at all; and

Jesus said, "I am the light of the world." If you look back over your own life, you will be certain to find that a great many of your troubles arose through no intentional fault of yours but through your ignorance or inexperience, or through your want of realizing to the full the implication of some situation which you had to meet. In other words, you suffered through want of light. Well, here the Bible explains that the Divine Power in you will be your light, and that you can train yourself to utilize it as such at any time that you need it.

The Lord is the strength of my life. Having promised us light, the Psalm now goes on to promise strength or power. We are to have power to do whatever we need to do, to meet whatever we need to meet, to tackle any problem or difficulty that can present itself in our lives. We are, in fact, to be "endued with power from on high" and need no longer trust to our own inadequate efforts. God will show us at any time the meaning of anything that we require to understand, will show us at any juncture what it is we ought to do, and He will furnish us with Divine strength to do it.

This wonderful verse then sums up its great message in the word "salvation," which, of course, means all-round harmony and demonstration; and with the penetrating psychological skill so characteristic of the Bible when it deals with the soul of man, it obliges us to ask ourselves, point blank, what there is now to be afraid of. And anyone who accepts the premises will hardly have any trouble in reaching the conclusion that there is nothing to be afraid of, because God lives and reigns—and then the back of the trouble is already broken.

When the wicked, even mine enemies and my foes came upon me to eat up my flesh, they stumbled and fell.

Of course, "the wicked," and "mine enemies," as always in the Bible, stand for our own thoughts, for our fears and doubts of every kind; and truly indeed do they sometimes come upon us as though "to eat up our flesh"—most people have at some time or other been only too painfully conscious of the aptness of this telling simile—and here you are promised that they shall stumble and fall.

Though an host should encamp against me, my heart shall not fear: though war should rise against me, in this will I be confident.

Here the Psalmist reiterates his confidence and makes us, his readers, reiterate ours. He makes us say that our hearts shall not fear, and he makes us believe it too, and can you think of any more beautiful assurance in the world than just that one—"my heart shall not fear"? When you can say quietly and truthfully at any hour of the day or night "my heart shall shall not fear," the world has no more power over you—you are free. War of various kinds may rise up against you, but you will be confident, and therefore you will be victorious.

LIGHT AND SALVATION

One thing have I desired of the Lord, that will I seek after; that I may dwell in the house of the Lord all the days of my life, to behold the beauty of the Lord, and to enquire in his temple.

For in the time of trouble he shall hide me in his pavilion: in the secret of his tabernacle shall he hide me; he shall set me up upon a rock.

These two verses constitute a remarkable expression of what is often called the second birth. Briefly this means that a man or woman has taken the most important step that a human being can take, that vital step in comparison with which all other experiences are of relatively minor importance. The new birth or second birth, or what you may be pleased to call it, means that you clearly understand and definitely accept the fact that nothing matters except attunement with God. When you can honestly say, "I realize now that nothing in life really matters except that I get my conscious attunement with God

LIGHT AND SALVATION

—because when I have that, everything else will rightly follow, and until I do get that nothing else can be right—and I am going to make everything else secondary to that," then you have really experienced the new birth whether the realization itself has yet arrived or not. When you have reached that stage you do not allow any external happening really to grieve you, or frighten you, or hurt you very deeply, because you know that external things are but passing shadows of no permanent importance. And now because they cannot bind you they cannot hurt you, and so you are free. And above all you do not allow the delaying of the realization itself to fret you or discourage you in the least because you know the Truth, even if you do not feel it.

This steadfast determination to dwell in the house of the Lord, to behold His beauty and to learn His secrets, means that you are set upon a rock and that your house of life is secure (see Matthew 7, 24-27).

LIGHT AND SALVATION

And now shall mine head be lifted up above mine enemies round about me; therefore will I offer in his tabernacle sacrifices of joy; I will sing, yea, I will sing praises unto the Lord.

This verse closes the first section of the treatment with a burst of that praise and thanksgiving that is so powerful for demonstration. Singing in the Bible is always the supreme expression of joy and exaltation, as we know. We note here that to "have your head lifted above your enemies" is not merely a graphic figure of victory but is an important metaphysical symbol. The head is the bodily expression for man's power of knowing Divine Truth —his Christ faculty we call it—and it is, of course, by an increase of understanding that we overcome limitation.

Hear, O Lord, when I cry with my voice: have mercy also upon me, and answer me.

When thou saidst, Seek ye my face; my heart said unto thee, Thy face, Lord, will I seek.

LIGHT AND SALVATION

Hide not thy face far from me; put not thy servant away in anger: thou hast been my help; leave me not, neither forsake me, O God of my salvation.

When my father and my mother forsake me, then the Lord will take me up.

The Psalmist here employs the dramatic form of addressing God. This gives the prayer vividness and intensity; but he is really affirming that God does hear us when we "cry with our voice" or "speak the Word," as we would say. He goes on to claim in different ways that God answers prayer. The actual affirmative form is usually the most effective form for healing a definite condition; but do not hesitate to address God when you feel so inclined. Do not abandon *any* kind of prayer In fact, do not give up anything in your religious life that you find to be helpful This Christ Truth comes to us not to destroy but to fulfill; not to rob us of anything good, but to give us more and more of the All-Good.

LIGHT AND SALVATION

Seek ye my face. Of course, this does not mean that God has a limited, material face like a man or woman. It is a well known symbol. It is true that in many of the great classical pictures, God is represented as a man—usually a man round about sixty years of age, and wearing a beard. But this was a well understood artistic convention. A man at that age was assumed to have attained the maximum degree of wisdom, and so it was really a symbolical way of expressing Divine Wisdom. The face, in fact, symbolizes the power of recognition. In everyday life it is by the face that we recognize people, not usually by their hands or feet, for example, and to seek the face of God means to seek a recognition of God's Presence to the point of realization, so that we "know" Him by experiencing Him. When we find a difficulty in getting our spiritual contact, it is as though God had hidden His face. Of course, God never does that, but we allow a veil of selfishness, doubt, and fear to come between us and Him. People

LIGHT AND SALVATION

sometimes speak of the sun having "gone in" when they really mean that a cloud has come between the sun and them, but, of course, everyone knows that the sun is shining unchanged on the other side of the cloud.

The Psalmist now strongly affirms this fact that God cannot and will not "hide His face" from His children, and he drives his point home by saying that even if his father and mother were to desert him, God would not do so. In the Orient where the family link is so strong that it overrides all private and personal considerations, this is a very telling statement indeed.

In other words, this section of the treatment shows us that doubts and fears may assail the Psalmist in the midst of his prayer—as they assail us all at times—but that he meets and vanquishes them in the scientific way.

Teach me thy way, O Lord, and lead me in a plain path, because of mine enemies.

LIGHT AND SALVATION

Deliver me not over unto the will of mine enemies; for false witnesses are risen up against me, and such as breathe out cruelty.

The Psalmist now prays for spiritual understanding and for peace of mind. The enemies, as always, are his own fears, and these fears take their rise in the fact that "false witnesses" rise up and confront him. And no one who has been through this experience will doubt the appropriateness of that telling phrase that our fears are things "such as breathe out cruelty." Verily, doubt and fear are the cruelest things that can come into the life of man.

I had fainted, unless I had believed to see the goodness of the Lord in the land of the living.

Wait on the Lord; be of good courage, and he shall strengthen thine heart: wait, I say, on the Lord.

Here, the Psalmist, following up the rhythmical play and interplay of thought, characteristic of the Bible, once more makes it clear to his own mind that his reliance is indeed entirely upon the Divine Power, and not upon his own limited resources, his intellect, or his will power, for instance. He says that unless he had believed God would perform the necessary miracle, he would not have expected it to happen at all.

The closing phrase is a powerful exhortation to be active and steadfast in prayer—that you ought always to pray and not to faint. To "wait upon the Lord" does not in the least mean neglecting a problem in the hope that God will come along and solve it for you. It means intensifying spiritual activity. Waiting on the Lord means praying constantly and systematically about your problem. The effect of this will be to "strengthen your heart," which means that you will receive encouragement and power to continue your prayers; and that your consciousness will be gradually changed until your problem melts away altogether in the realization of restored harmony and peace. Thus does God answer prayer.

No Results Without Prayer

THERE is only one method of spiritual progress, and that is by the Practice of the Presence of God, whether we call this Scientific Prayer or Spiritual Treatment. There is no other way. Mankind is continually seeking to discover a short cut of some kind or other, because the carnal mind is constitutionally lazy; but as usual the lazy man takes the most pains in the long run, and having wasted his time in wandering up by-paths, he is ultimately driven by failure and suffering to the realization of the grand truth that *there is no substitute for prayer.*

This does not mean that any particular form of prayer is essential, but prayer there must be; that is, the conscious dwelling upon the Being of God. I have heard people say: "I did not treat when such a problem arose; I just knew the Truth about it, and the trouble disappeared." But this, of course, is exactly what scientific prayer or treatment is, and in its most beautiful and effective form. Such a person really means that he has not used some rigid or crystallized form of expression, which, needless to say, is not in the least essential. Formal or set treatments are useful things to have by one, to fall back upon when spontaneity fails. Then they help to focus the thought, and usually set the natural well a-bubbling. But the thought's the thing, and the simpler and more spontaneous it is, and the more quickly it comes the better.

If your intuitive nature is well developed, you will seldom need to use formal statements at all. This is excellent—for who will trouble to climb a ladder when he is strong enough to leap over the wall? Unfortunately, however, there are a great many people with little or no intuitional development as yet, and many other people lose the ability to receive intuitional messages when worried or frightened. Then the ladder will probably be their salvation.

It must not be overlooked that very many people actually do all their work with formal statements of Truth, and get consistently good results by working in this way. Not through repeating affirmations like a parrot, it is needless to say. Those who work like a parrot inevitably make the parrot's demonstration—they remain in the cage. Of a good worker who used the same phrases many times it was said by a friend: "He constantly uses the old affirmations, but he stuffs them with fresh feeling every time." For one who has neither very much intuitional power at his command, nor yet the ability easily to express his thoughts in words, this is a model procedure. Meanwhile, in such a case the student must be particularly careful not to accept his want of intuitional power as a fixed thing, but to recognize it merely as a temporary disability to be gradually overcome. In fact, such a person should make a special point of treating himself for intuitional power regularly every day—by claiming it, of course—*I have conscious Divine Intelligence. I individualize Omniscience. I have direct knowledge of Truth. I have perfect intuition. I have spiritual perception. I know.*

Thus we see that practically all students of Truth do in fact employ treatment in one form or another, even though they may disclaim it. There are, however, a few people who actually refrain from all treatment on principle, but since one has never heard of their healing anyone, and they seem to be continually in personal difficulties of all sorts, the facts speak for themselves, and only go to prove the rule that treatment, or the Practice of the Presence of God, is the only road to harmony.

The Garden of Allah
Isaiah 35

EVEN those who love the Bible most are apt to make the mistake of looking upon it as merely a book, the greatest book ever written, no doubt, but still a book; whereas the truth about the Bible is that it is really a spiritual vortex in which spiritual power pours from the Absolute or Divine Plane into the physical plane or plane of manifestation.

But the Bible is not only the great source of spiritual truth, it is also the greatest collection of literary masterpieces that we possess. Almost every literary form is represented in the Bible, both in prose and poetry. History, biography, philosophy, the short story in its perfection—re-read some of the parables, for example—the epic, and even that supposedly modern form, the novel, are all found there. The Book of Job is really a play; and Revelation is a drama in form so strange and unprecedented that it remains in its entirety almost incomprehensible to most people, however much they may appreciate its separate details.

Above all, the Bible abounds in beautiful and powerful prayers or treatments, and this alone makes it for us the most important book in the world. This is because prayer is really the only thing that matters. The only way in which man can improve himself or his conditions, get a better knowledge of God—save his soul, in short—is by prayer. Prayer indeed is the only real action there is; that is to say, it is the only action that makes things different.

Whenever you pray, you change your soul for the better. If the prayer is very short or the degree of realization very poor, the change it brings about may be small, but it occurs. It could not by any chance happen under any circumstances that any man or woman could pray for a single moment without some result for good following. Whenever you pray, your whole subsequent life is, as a consequence, somewhat different from what it would have been had you not prayed.

Now prayer is the only thing that does change the *quality* of the soul. Any other activity may make a *quantitative* change in the soul by adding experience, or by extending one's fund of knowledge; but it does not change the quality. Only prayer does that, and it is the quality of one's soul that determines his destiny.

As long as there is no qualitative change in your soul, you will, under any given circumstances, say or do the thing that such a person as you are would say or do in such a case, because we never really act out of character. We are never other than ourselves. When we try to be other than ourselves by an effort of human will, we are just being ourselves all the more on that account. When you pray, however, you by that act become at least a slightly different man and, therefore, all your subsequent activities are different too. So prayer is the only thing that matters.

The word "treatment" is a technical term that many of us use for prayer that is directed to the overcoming of a specific, practical difficulty, and the Bible is full of prayers and treatments of every kind.

When you find yourself in any kind of trouble, no matter what it may be, whether you think it is caused by somebody else's conduct, or whether you feel that it is your own fault, or whether it seems to be no one's fault; in any case the only possible thing to do is to treat yourself about it. If you give yourself an efficient treatment—or it may be that several treatments will be necessary—then the difficulty, whatever it is, will presently disappear and you will find yourself out of your trouble. In other words, your prayer will be "answered," or, as we often say, you will make your demonstration.

A STUDY IN TREATMENT

But what is a treatment? Well, briefly, a treatment means that you recollect and realize the Truth about God until you have brought about a change in your own consciousness, whereupon, as a result of this change in yourself, the outer things completely change too. Note particularly that this does not mean merely that you gain courage or fortitude to meet your difficulties in a new spirit. That would be better than nothing, but not much better. The tremendous fact is that prayer does change things. As a consequence of the change in your mentality that results from your treatment, outer conditions change completely. Other people change their conduct and their attitude toward you. Unpleasant things that would otherwise have happened do not happen, and good things that would not have happened had you not prayed, do happen—brought about by prayer alone. *Prayer does change things.*

Now how is the necessary change in

consciousness to be brought about? Or, in other words, how is a treatment made? Well the first thing to realize is that merely repeating a form of words is seldom any use at all. (That is better than nothing if you should be so frightened or worried that you cannot do anything more. In fact, to cling to a single phrase may be the only thing that can save you in a great emergency; but fortunately such an extreme condition is very exceptional.) It is the change in feeling and conviction that matters. Any means that brings this about—and whatever means does it most quickly—is the best treatment. Whatever will raise your consciousness from the lower level of trouble to the higher level of freedom is a treatment. In many cases the quiet, thoughtful repetition of certain affirmations of Truth is sufficient, such as: "I am surrounded by the Love and Peace of God"; or "Divine Intelligence opens my way." Sometimes, and especially if

A STUDY IN TREATMENT

you are faithful in daily prayer and meditation, the mere momentary "feeling out" for God will clear the most formidable difficulty with lightning-like rapidity; feeling out in thought, that is to say, without formulating any words at all. The reading of a page of any spiritual book that appeals to you or, above all, a few verses or a chapter from the Bible often constitutes a most powerful treatment. It is for this reason that the Bible has so many prayers and treatments included in its pages.

The literary arrangement in which we have received our Bible is very misleading in many instances. The divisions into chapters and verses was made comparatively recently. The original writers had nothing whatever to do with it, and it was done in an arbitrary fashion that paid very little attention to the subject matter concerned. So it happens that with a writer, such as Isaiah, for instance, his works have been run together with little

THE GARDEN OF ALLAH

or no regard to sequence of subject or chronological order, and then, so to speak, chopped up into approximately equal lengths which are called chapters. In addition to this, a great deal of material, splendid in itself but not belonging to the prophet called Isaiah, has been included. Of course this makes no practical difference at all, as long as we know about it. The actual writer of anything in the Bible does not matter in the least, because the true author of it all is the Holy Spirit.

One of the greatest prayers or treatments ever written is included among the writings of Isaiah, and is known to us as Chapter 35. This chapter number, as we have seen, is purely an arbitrary designation. The chapter itself has nothing in particular to do with either Chapter 34 or Chapter 36. That number has no more intrinsic significance than the number a book may bear on the shelf of a library. As this chapter constitutes a particularly beautiful and effective treatment for any purpose, we shall now consider it at some length.

The first thing we notice is that in its literary form it is a glorious poetic rhapsody. The writer, in contemplating the wonder and the love of God, rises to a white heat of spiritual exaltation. The leaden shoes of fear and doubt that glue man to the earth in his everyday life are cast aside, and he rises on the pinions of Divine Inspiration into the region where all his petty limitations and handicaps vanish in the splendor of the Divine Presence. For the time being he leaves behind him every small and mean thing that keeps a man from God, from joy and freedom. And as he has succeeded in enshrining this transcendent experience in words that still live and glow today with much of his own original divine ecstasy, it becomes possible for us in using this prayer with spiritual understanding, to kindle our own torch from the same fire, and, if we can tune ourselves in with his note, to transcend also any particular difficulty or group of difficulties that may be oppressing us.

The wilderness and the solitary place shall be glad for them; and the desert shall rejoice, and blossom as the rose. The first thing that strikes us here is that the writer is, of course, as all Bible writers are, an Oriental, and therefore he will give his message in the language and idiom of the Orient. This is so obvious that it would be unnecessary to mention it did we not know how many European and American people down to the last generation were in the habit of taking every Oriental simile and flourish at its face value, and often trying to apply it with the utmost literalness to some condition of life in London, or Mancester, or Chicago.

He begins his prayer in the best possible way that a prayer can begin, by a splendid act of faith in God. Always be-

A STUDY IN TREATMENT

gin your prayers with an act of faith. Remember that Jesus tells us that faith in the Love of God will literally move mountains. And so our Oriental Prophet starts with what is doubtless the greatest affirmation of faith in God of which an Oriental is capable. He looks to God and cries: *The wilderness and the solitary place shall be glad . . . and the desert shall rejoice and blossom as the rose.* Think of it; the Oriental desert to become a garden, to blossom as a rose, to be a center of prosperity and riches. Nothing in our human experience can seem on the face of it less probable than this. No human trouble could be more difficult than this problem of turning the desert into a smiling garden. But with God all things are possible, absolutely all things, anything; and so to Him the redemption of a desert wilderness is just as easy as anything else.

The Bible is predominantly the book of a desert people. Always as the great drama of the Bible story moves across the stage of time, we are conscious of the desert as the background against which it moves. Palestine, a narrow strip of land not much bigger than Wales, was hemmed in by a desert on three sides, and by the unfamiliar and to them unattractive sea on the fourth. Almost everything that came into Palestine came across a desert. Goods and merchandise made their slow way in the leisurely desert caravans. All visitors who came to that country came through the desert and arrived wearied and parched with its sand and dust; and any new ideas that might filter into the world of Palestine had to filter through the desert too, and would inevitably arrive, like the travelers themselves, bearing about them something of the same desert atmosphere. For, just as to people living in the British Isles the sea is always the background —it is the sea that has moulded their history, and conditions their everyday

A STUDY IN TREATMENT

lives, even though they may live so far from the ocean that they have never seen it—so the people of Palestine though they might never venture into the wilderness itself, were shaped and governed from first to last by the eternal, unchanging desert, and the conditions of life that spring from a desert home. Always the desert haunted them. There is not a page in the Bible in which we do not vaguely sense the eternal sands and hear the distant tinkle of the camel bells.

And so for us of the West it calls for a distinct effort of the imagination truly to appreciate this splendid declaration with which the poet opens his prayer. He takes the one condition above all others with which man had been totally unable to deal, much less to conquer—the desert; the one condition perhaps which would seem to him as an Oriental to be eternal and unchangeable, the one condition, we may say, that it would be utterly hopeless to think of changing:

and he declares that the goodness and love of God shall completely conquer this. How complete and thorough that conquest is to be is signified by piling up, in the Eastern way, symbol upon symbol —*it shall rejoice and blossom as the rose* —one of the richest and most splendid of God's creations, calling for a special quality of soil and particular care in its culture.

It shall blossom abundantly, and rejoice even with joy and singing: the glory of Lebanon shall be given unto it, the excellency of Carmel and Sharon, they shall see the glory of the Lord, and the excellency of our God. On and on he goes in pursuit of his great theme. The glory of the desert redeemed is to be in proportion to its former barrenness. It shall rejoice with joy and singing. Glory of every kind shall be heaped upon it, the especial glory that the Poet knew in his time as only to be found among the cedars of Lebanon; the austere grandeur

A STUDY IN TREATMENT

that he felt only in Carmel; and the sweet, fragrant peace that he had known among the beautifully kept gardens of Sharon. He closes this first stanza, his opening declaration of faith, by reaffirming *They shall see the glory of the Lord, and the excellency of our God.*

In reading this carefully we begin to catch something of the Prophet's own divine faith in the goodness of God, and as faith is infectious, we find the power of his understanding gradually fanning our tiny spark of it into a flame.

Below each level of thought in the Bible there always lies yet a deeper level for those who can find it, and so it is here. Lebanon, Carmel, and Sharon in detail stand for certain spiritual faculties in the soul of man that gradually develop as he persists along the pathway of spiritual awakening, and the Prophet here implies, for those who can understand, that these definite spiritual gifts are the outcome of such prayers as this. Of course, the desert or wilderness is a general term for any kind of trouble or difficulty. It may be a specific problem that you have to overcome, or, in the wider sense, the general state of feeling cut off from God, of which we are all so conscious to our sorrow.

It is interesting to note that, in a very wonderful and different sense, the desert may be taken to symbolize that state of mind in which man has attained to a high degree of concentration upon God. Sooner or later you will have to put God first in your life, that is to say, your own true spiritual development must become the only thing that really matters. It need not, perhaps had better not, be the only thing in your life, but it must be the first thing. When this happens you will find that you have got rid of a great deal of the unnecessary junk that most people carry about; mental junk, of course, although physical junk is very apt to follow upon this. You will find that

A STUDY IN TREATMENT

you will do a great deal less running about after things that do not matter and only waste your time and energy, when once you have put God first. Your life will become simpler and quieter, but in the true sense, richer and infinitely more worth while.

This has usually happened in the desert. The true desert wanderer has few physical possessions, none of our artificial needs, and few of our so-called comforts; yet he is among the happiest of the human race. Commonly he fears nothing in life or in death. It was an Arab sitting at the door of his tent at night, free from the burden of useless possessions, his mind and heart clarified by simple living, who gazed up at the myriad golden stars so bright in the eastern sky; looked about him with uninterrupted gaze to the distant dusky horizon; and said, "The desert is the garden of Allah."

Strengthen ye the weak hands, and con-

firm the feeble knees. Say to them that are of a fearful heart, Be strong, fear not: behold, your God will come with vengeance, even God with a recompense; he will come and save you. The first stanza of this wonderful poem-prayer having led the reader to make a splendid declaration of faith, this, the second stanza, takes up definitely the task of working upon his consciousness direct. It says *strengthen ye the weak hands.* Here we meet one of the most important symbols to be found in the Bible—the hand. The hand, briefly, stands for the power of manifestation, or the capacity to express God's ideas on the physical plane. It is the power of getting things done. It is the power of making demonstrations, as we say, or of getting answers to prayer, and so the expression, *strengthen ye the weak hands,* is a command that we are to rise up out of limitation, refuse to put up with it, and insist upon harmony and freedom; that, in fact, we ought always to pray and not to faint. Jesus has told us by means of two separate parables that we are not to accept less than harmony; that we are to go on praying until we make our demonstration; that we are not to take "no" for an answer. And here the inspired writer teaches the same lesson. You should never "put up" with anything. You should never be content to accept less than harmony, peace, and freedom. Until you get these things you must be insistent in prayer.

This particular symbol is a very interesting one. Man is, in his true nature, a spiritual being, a spark from the Divine Fire, but this divine spark, the I Am, has to be embodied, and the human body with which we are familiar, which we all carry about with us, is really but an embodiment of the various faculties and capacities of the Divine I Am. Actually we are at present seeing this embodiment in a very, very limited way, even in the case of the most healthy and beautiful bodies; nevertheless that is what it is. The Real Self, or I Am, has the power of manifesting absolutely any idea or set of ideas which it can understand, even to some extent; and this power we see embodied as the hand. In all ages the hand has been understood symbolically in this way. We speak of a thing being handy. A person who performs all sorts of essential business for another is often spoken of as his "right hand." At banquets the guest of honor is placed at the right hand of the host. The Christ Truth "sitteth at the right hand of God, the Father Almighty"—it is the Christ nature that manifests God through man. The word for hand, in Latin, is *manus* and this is derived originally from a Sanskrit word meaning the thinker. Our English word "man" ultimately derives from the same root and carries the same implicit meaning. And we know that it is man's *raison d'être* to manifest God.

A STUDY IN TREATMENT

Man the manifestor is or should be the hand of God through which God works, and this he is through his power of thought, because he is essentially a thinker. When we wish to paralyze a man's activities we handcuff him, thereby putting his hands out of action, and to have both hands amputated is reckoned as almost complete disablement.

Confirm the feeble knees. This is a very obvious figure for getting rid of fear. There are not many of the sons of men who have not at some time or other known what it was to feel their knees almost literally going from under them through nervousness or fear. Such a condition, unless overcome, is the prelude to the total collapse of the body in what we call a faint. Now when people are in grave difficulties and are beginning to lose their courage—and to lose courage is to lose all—the soul may very aptly be described as being in this condition. The Prophet therefore strikes boldly at our weak hands and feeble knees and proceeds to confirm them, or make them firm, by bringing to mind the truth about God. One might well say indeed that essentially Scientific Prayer or Treatment is just this thing of pausing to *recollect the truth about God*. We do not try to do something with our prayers in the sense of seeking to manipulate things to our liking. Such a proceeding would be will power and not prayer, but we pause in the current of material things and *recollect* what we know to be the truth about God. This acceptation and reaffirmation of the Truth is what brings a spiritual demonstration.

The Prophet says with unanswerable simplicity: *Behold, your God will come with vengeance, even God with a recompense; he will come and save you.* And why? Because you are saying your prayers. Because, instead of being carried away in the tide of difficulty as the "heathen" or non-pray-er is, you have paused to recollect the truth about God. You have made the magnificent declaration of faith in the first stanza, and so the action of God will now come into your life with vengeance or vindication.

People sometimes wonder why a loving God should allow them to get into trouble at all in the first place, or why He does not help them without waiting for their prayers. The answer is that we have free will. This is the most precious of all things for us because it is our identity in God as the I Am. If God were to interfere in our lives without our having called upon Him through prayer, our free will would be abrogated, and we should lose our identity. Actually this could not happen, because it would be against the Law of Being. We have to know here that this word "vengeance" in the Bible is a technical term meaning *vindication*. Needless to say, God, Infinite Mind, is not capable of approaching anything like what is known among men as revenge. What happens is that the action of God following upon your prayer *vindicates* the Law of Being, and as this Law is the law of perfect good you are saved. The demonstration may figuratively be described as the recompense for your treatment.

Then the eyes of the blind shall be opened, and the ears of the deaf shall be unstopped. Then shall the lame man leap as an hart, and the tongue of the dumb sing: for in the wilderness shall waters break out, and streams in the desert. These two phrases constitute one of the most wonderful passages in the whole Bible. There is no other that can quite be put beside it. It is a song of triumph, and joy, and liberation, probably the most glorious celebration of the power of God in prayer that ever was written. Think what it promises, what it announces to be the natural result of spiritual prayer: The eyes of the blind shall be opened, and the ears of the deaf shall be unstopped, the lame man shall leap as an hart, and the tongue of the dumb shall sing! Is this a sufficient manifesto of spiritual healing? Is anything of importance left out? Can we, in the face of this, declare that any physical condition is beyond the reach of prayer? Can we dare say or think any more that with God some things are possible, and some things are not? The blind, the deaf, the dumb, and the crippled are to be set free and restored to health by the power of God.

Physical healing is one of the most glorious manifestations of the Universal Christ. It is the Beautiful Gate of the Temple, but it is not everything. It is the spiritual gift that has been most emphasized in the metaphysical movement for two or three generations, but as Paul was careful to imply in his enumeration, it is only one gift. The healing of the body is essential, but the thing that really matters of course is the spiritual development of the soul. What is a physical healing but the outer evidence that a step in spiritual development has been taken; and the physical healings enumerated here fully and beautifully as they apply to the physical body, are still more important when raised to a higher level.

It is glorious that the physical eyes of the physically blind should be opened, but the physical eyes also symbolize man's power of spiritual perception; and the magnificent promise of these two verses particularly implies that the gift of spiritual perception is to be acquired by prayer; and that when we earnestly pray for it nothing can prevent our getting it.

It is glorious that the ears of the physically deaf should be unstopped; but hearing, on the higher level, stands for spiritual understanding, and it is ten times more important that spiritually obtuse people should obtain an understanding of the truth about God and about life.

It is glorious that the physically crippled should regain his strength so that, throwing away his crutches and straightening his back, he shall assume the birthright of healthy manhood and run and leap like a deer. But it is ten times more important that moral and spiritual cripples should succeed in surmounting their infirmities and rise up in the free exercise of spiritual faculty and prayer.

It is glorious that the physically dumb should acquire the power of the physical word to speak and sing; but the tongue stands also for man's spiritual dominion or power, and it is a thousand times more important for the spiritually dumb, those men and women who have no power of spiritual demonstration, to acquire the power of the Logos or Creative Word which is their divine inheritance, and learn to use it with telling effect for themselves and others.

Never before or since has the importance of these things both physical and spiritual been brought home so convincingly to men's hearts as here. And by way of a final emphasis on these transcendent truths the Oriental Prophet repeats his supreme argument: *For in the wilderness shall waters break out, and streams in the desert. And the parched ground shall become a pool, and the thirsty land springs of water.* To the Oriental reader no claim for Divine Power could seem to out-reach this.

As we have seen, the sandy desert is to him the one eternal and unchanging fact, and to say that it shall be plenteously filled with water is to include all promises. We need to remember that, in that Eastern land, water is considered the most precious of all substances; comparatively small quantities are often transported miles upon miles upon the backs of camels and mules, and in remote desert places a cup of water is literally worth its weight in gold—far more perhaps, for it may mean the difference between life and death. We in the West who seldom know a real shortage of water, whose climate is, if anything, a trifle too wet for comfort, have to use our imagination again in order that we may realize how powerful and telling this simile really is, and all that it conveys of the power, and majesty, and resources, and love of God.

In the habitation of dragons, where each lay, shall be grass with reeds and rushes. As the result of prayer, of the recollection of the Omnipresence of God, and the affirmation of faith in His goodness, we are to lose our fear; regain our power of manifesting harmony and peace; obtain our physical healing, no matter what the malady may have been; and, above all, we are to develop spiritual perception, spiritual understanding, the power of speaking the Word with effect, and to acquire the capacity to develop new spiritual faculties altogether, for which there are no words in ordinary language. (We are but lame men without these faculties.) And now the Prophet says significantly: *In the habitation of dragons, where each lay, shall be grass with reeds and rushes.* This is a very remarkable and significant statement. The writer of this wonderful treatment knew all there is to be known about human nature. Our psychological experts are just beginning to scratch the surface of this subject; nevertheless much good work has been done by what is called the new psychology, in spite of its manifest errors; and people are just beginning to realize the existence of those "dark unfathomed caves" of our nature that are nowadays called the subconscious mind. We are beginning to realize that a thought is not dead or powerless merely because we are not consciously thinking it; but that it has simply floated out of sight under the ice, as it were, carrying with it all the potentialities that it had for evil, and much more in addition, now that it is out of sight. We are beginning to understand that a thing is not destroyed because it is suppressed, but, on the contrary, just as compression increases tremendously the detonating power of an explosive, so thoughts and feelings, and especially feelings that for one reason or another we do not care to face frankly, acquire an incalculable access of power for evil when they are suppressed into the subconscious and become what we call complexes. Indeed, psychotherapeutics has proved that a very large share of all our temporal ills spring from these very things. Now, Isaiah knew all this, and his name for these complexes is *dragons,* and a very good name too. It would be difficult to find a better one. And here he promises that as a result of prayer the dragons shall be cleared out and destroyed, and the watery depths where each lay shall become a secure and peaceful mead—quiet with grass and reeds and rushes.

And an highway shall be there, and a way, and it shall be called The way of holiness. We now come to one of the transcendent revelations of the Bible. For sheer power and splendor this passage stands alone. The whole stanza is quite unmatched either in scripture or elsewhere. The Prophet rises higher and higher on the inspirational tide that bears him onward as he envisions the complete salvation of mankind that shall be. His eye sweeps along the whole flood of spiritual evolution, right on to the uttermost bounds where the human and the Divine shall be merged in final Unity.

For the individual, too, it is the promise and the means for the triumphant journey back to God. It is the great manifesto of salvation, the complete statement of the way of escape from limitation, sin, sickness, and death.

And an highway shall be there, and a way, and it shall be called The way of holiness. This is a definite and, one may say, businesslike statement that there is to be a way out. It means that it is no longer to be necessary for man to put up with anything less than perfect harmony. It really means that resignation to anything less than peace, health, and harmony—so far from being a virtue—will be known as what it actually is, a breach of the Law of Being. Let us make no mistake about this. Now that this way has been opened, resignation to limitation and inharmony is nothing but a fine name for laziness and cowardice. The Prophet definitely says that there shall be a highway. Now what is a highway? Is it not a public main road, accessible to everybody, which all those who observe the law use with equal right. No one has any authority to put a barrier on the highway, to fence it off to the exclusion of certain people, or to exercise any kind of proprietary rights whatever. That is what a highway is, and the Prophet here definitely says that the Path of freedom and salvation is to be a highway. No man, no organization, no rules and regulations of either the dead or the living, have any power or authority whatever to forbid anyone to that highway, or to make any terms upon which he shall enter it. No conditions of membership, no entrance fees or entrance ceremonials have any authority from the inspired word. It is public. It is open. It is free.

Having prophesied a highway, the writer then definitely states that it will be a Way. Now a "way," of course, is a technical term meaning a way back to the consciousness of the Real Presence of God. It is what we often call the Path. And we may pause for a moment here to realize the tremendous importance of the statement that the Path is a *highway*. Most religious movements, at any rate the older and greater ones, have taught of the Path and how to enter upon it. But always they treated it,

A STUDY IN TREATMENT

not as a highway, but as a private road fenced in by themselves, to the gates of which they alone held the keys. The Bible, however, came to the world to break down this exclusiveness and to say that the Way is a highway. It is really impossible for the student to overstress the importance of this fact. Again and again and again throughout history the open highway has been given to the people for a short time, only to be closed up again, and before very long, and usually by the very people who had opened it. So grave are the dangers that attend organized religion, so powerful and so subtle are the evils resulting from the accumulation of much property (an evil which overtakes almost every well organized church sooner or later), that unless we keep this point constantly fresh in our minds, we may be in danger of repeating the old mistakes.

The Prophet goes on to say that the Way or the Path is the path of holiness.

Now, of course, we need to understand that the Bible uses the word holiness in a very much wider and more far-reaching sense than the usual one. The word "holiness" really means wholeness, not just holiness of character, rare and wonderful as that is, but complete holiness of life. This includes perfect bodily health—no invalid is holy in the Bible sense, however spiritual he may be in other respects—it includes the idea of happiness or true peace of mind, of prosperity, which means freedom from nagging fears concerning the necessaries of life; in fact, holiness means all-round health, prosperity, and spiritual harmony. Actually the words whole, holy, wholesome, heal, and healing, all go back to the same old English root, because they are but different aspects of the same thing.

This does not in the least detract from the transcendent importance of what is usually designated holiness, the thing to which a great modern Rationalist referred sadly when he said "Holiness, deepest of all words that defy definition."

The Prophet goes on to say of this glorious highway, *the unclean shall not pass over it.* Now exactly what does this mean? Too often it has been supposed to imply that the ordinary human being, full of faults and shortcomings, and, still more, one conscious of graver sin, has no chance upon that highway; that it is reserved for the saint and the spiritual hero—for those who are indeed clean. Yet nothing could possibly be farther from the truth. What point could there be in providing a highway for those who are already "saved." Did not our Lord say, "The well need not a physician, but those who are sick." And indeed to suppose otherwise would be like saying that one should not use soap until his hands were clean. The fact is, you do not bring a clean heart to God that He may love you for it; you bring your unclean heart to Him in order that He may cleanse it. The real meaning of this magnificent statement, the real bearing of this whole glorious final stanza, is that the highway shall be provided for the average human being, the "wayfaring man," you and me who stand in need of purification and salvation. The "unclean" are those very thoughts and beliefs of limitation, sin, sickness, fear, doubt, and so forth, that are the only things keeping us out of the Kingdom of Heaven today. These are the unclean; and once we are upon that highway they have no more power to hinder our progress. Their power of keeping us back in the darkness is gone.

No longer need frail, weak human beings fear to approach the highway. *It shall be for those.*

The wayfaring men, though fools, shall not err therein. Having shown that no degree of weakness or guilt can keep a man off the Path, if he really wants to enter upon it, Isaiah here takes up the other point that no lack of intellectual power or intellectual training can exclude him either. No want of what is called cleverness, or what is generally called education, makes any difference here. The most brilliant academic career, and the simplest unlettered background, are equally unimportant, provided there is the right intention, reinforced by right application. As a matter of fact, intellectual brilliance and much secular knowledge have kept many people off of this Path because, under our modern system of education, these things are very apt to beget spiritual pride. On the other hand, a good sound intelligence, while not in the least a guarantee of spiritual power, is likely to be very helpful in spiritual development, because it enables the candidate to appreciate the need for thoroughness, faithfulness, and disinterestedness; and it leads him to check up his results in order to insure that he really is making progress as time goes on. It saves him from living in a fool's paradise by supposing that he is demonstrating when he is not. It enables him to distinguish between spiritual progress and mere emotional indulgence. The great point is that we do not have to bring knowledge or wisdom to the Path, but that it is the function of the Path to equip us with these things.

No lion shall be there, nor any ravenous beast shall go up thereon, it shall not be found there; but the redeemed shall walk there. Here the whole story is repeated in another form, in accordance with the Eastern poetical tradition, which drives home its points by means of variety of iteration. Once upon the Path, troubles and difficulties will indeed still come to us, for a time at least; but now they come up from the inside, so to say; they emerge from the depths of our own personality, because they have no business to be there, and are to be dealt with once and for all. No longer are they lions or ravenous beasts from which we need to be protected; but rather are they problems to be solved once and for all, that we may be free forever.

And now this wonderful poem finishes up with one of the supreme verses of the whole Bible. Having entered and walked the Path, learned the lessons, and won the crown of completed understanding, our limitations and our spectral fears—for spectres they are, that and nothing more—disappear forever; and the glory of the Union, the grand transformation, is completed. Old things are passed away and *the ransomed of the Lord return, and come to Zion with songs and everlasting joy upon their heads: they shall obtain joy and gladness, and sorrow and sighing shall flee away.* Did ever man write like this? The "ransomed of the Lord" are of course those who have realized, not merely believed, but realized their oneness with their own Indwelling Christ; realized that that Indwelling

Christ is in reality and truth themselves, not near to, not belonging to, but identical with themselves. Such are they who really have demonstrated the I Am.

And they shall return and come to Zion. Zion is the direct realization of God. Jerusalem is the highest thing in the human consciousness less than the Divine contact, but Zion is the realization of God Himself. It is to this that the Souls Triumphant will come, and, says the poet, with songs and everlasting joy upon their heads. They are to come singing, he says, and this is significant, for a spontaneous song is our natural expression of the highest joy. The instinct of the human soul which has not been cramped by taboos and inhibitions is to burst into song when it feels happy and free; and so the Bible rightly uses the idea of singing to express utter and spontaneous joy. And note that it says "everlasting" joy, no joy that may fade away with the lapse of time or the coming of some unexpected cloud. This joy is to be the joy of God, that never can and never will wane when once we have found it. So precise and thorough is the Bible's expounding of the way of man's salvation that here it makes a point of putting the joy upon their heads. Now the human head symbolizes always the Christ understanding of Truth, as distinct from mere blind faith, or simple emotional groping; and so here we see that this divine joy is to be the joy of perfect *understanding,* which is the only real guarantee of permanence.

Our poem terminates its glorious upward sweep with a final clinching assurance, much as one might comfort a doubting child, an assurance that all this is really true, saying in the simplest language: *Sorrow and sighing shall flee away.*

Other Twice Born Books

When Man Listens
When man listens is an Oxford Group book. *It is an excellent guide on how to live a life of guidance by God.* The book outlines the principles that were followed by the Oxford Group. Many of these principles guide the Members of Alcoholics Anonymous and other 12 step programs

Twice Born Men
Twice born men Is about the Salvation Army and its effect on the lives of men who were considered the lowest of the low. Bad men, down trodden, and who were filled with fear. *It is also about men who had a conversion and became men who listened to God for guidance.* These men became happy, helpful people who sought to save others. They became members of the Army.

Life Changers
Life Changers is about the early work by Frank Buchman. How he changed the lives of the young men at Oxford University by helping them to find and Follow God's will. The men at Oxford went on to spread Franks work throughout the world. It became the most impactful Christian movement of the 20th Century. It became commonly known as the Oxford Group movement. *The cofounders of A.A. were members of this group and much of the A.A. principles came directly from it*

Inspired Children
The personal story of Olive Jones (Former president of the National Education association) true stories of how teaching Sunday School Children brought her faith. She also proved that teaching the young children 4 to 10 the principles of the Oxford Group, and that they too could find God. We have a great lesson of hope that children can and do find God if they are guided rightly.

To drink or not to drink
" *The Common Sense of Drinking" is one of the first and still one of the best books on the subject of alcoholism.* It gives the reader a straightforward way of determining if drinking alcohol is a problem. It is a great first book to give to any person who may be questioning the effects of alcohol.

Twice born ministers
Twice born ministers, was written by Sam Shoemaker. The first question is what is a twice born Minister? Sam stated it well when he said " I believe that the proof that a Minister is twice born lies not in his compliance with any arbitrary prerequisite, but simply in the power to produce more twice born people" Second question is how does this book help the layperson? "A dozen men are saying to you, whether you are a minister or a layman, that great things happened to them which can also happen to you." The rebirth Of the Ministers occurred as a result of using the Oxford Group principles and practices. The same principles that were taught To Dr Bob and Bill W. while in the Group meetings. Bill had the privilege of working closely with the Author at Calvary Church.

The Foundations of A.A.
The foundations of A.A. are best expressed through a trilogy of books that were written over a period of 25 years by two movements. They demonstrate the principles of service by helping others, listening to and following the will of God. We start with- "Twice Born Men" True stories of

the conversion of the lowest of the low who came from one of the worst sections of London. The Principles and practices of the Salvation Army laid the footing on which the foundation was to be built. Then we move on to the early work of Frank Buchman, in England with the Oxford Students. It is about Frank's direct interaction with them. In the stories of their Rebirth and there bringing the message of faith throughout the world. Franks teachings became the guiding a principle of that was the cement to build the base. Finally we complete with Sam Shoemakers work at Calvary Church in New York City. Sam and His Oxford Group worker did the pouring of the cement to complete the foundation

The Genius of fellowship
By Samuel M. Shoemaker and Carl Tuchy Palmieri
"The Genius of Fellowship" was written in 1932 By Sam Shoemaker. *Bill W. the cofounder of A.A* stated that Sam was the third cofounder of A.A. that "He was one of the few without whose ministration A.A. could never have been born in the first place nor prospered since" "From his teachings, Dr Bob and I absorbed most of the principles of A.A. Our ideas of self-examination, acknowledgement of character defects, restitution for harms done, and working with others came straight from Sam" "He passed to us the spiritual keys by which so many of us have since been liberated".

Children of the second Birth
Children of the second birth were written in 1927 and are filled with stories of men and women who found God and recovered from various maladies.
The primary focus was on quiet time—finding God's will and helping others to do the same.

The Original 12 Step Book
Written In 1946, By Ed Webster (The little red Book) was the first guide used to help people do the twelve steps. It was approved by AA, promoted, by Dr Bob; Dr. Bob thought it was the best description of how to work the steps that had ever been written. He sent copies of it all over the U.S. and Canada with his recommendation. *Until Dr. Bob's death in 1950, he insisted that the New York A.A. office make copies of this book available for sale through their office. And it was offered for sale by AA prior to AA 12 & 12.* It remains as the clearest and easiest to understand guide.

Life Began Yesterday
"Life Began Yesterday" is one of the many stories of recovering alcoholics and their spiritual rebirth that occurred during the mid nineteen Thirties. Stephen foot found sobriety before Bill W and Dr Bob. Both Bill W and Dr Bob found Sobriety while members of the Oxford Group. Stephen Foot and Bill W both had the personal tutelage from Sam Shoemaker. Sam was the head of the Oxford Group movement In the United States. His book was so popular that it was translated into nine languages and issued in Braille.

For the sinner in you
The message in this book is clear. We are perfectly human and as Human beings we have used our self-will in ways that offend God. It gives a firsthand account of the recovery path that is common among men in recovery.
Following these simple principles brings peace, serenity, joy and love

There is a solution

"There is a solution" gets at the underlying reason why people have a drinking problem, and it states the drinking is not the problem.

The Big Bender
Much wanted book about a struggle with alcoholism by an early Alcoholics Anonymous and Oxford Group associate. Charles Clapp was an Oxford Grouper, who AA founder Bill W had helped get sober in October of 1935. Charles Clapp had also been working with Sam Shoemaker, but could not stay sober until he got help from Bill. "The Big Bender" relates that story. Clapp was from Bedford Hills. His book was written around 1937 read by many recovering alcoholics

The Game of Life
This prosperity classic was written in 1925 by Florence Scovil Shinn. <u>It stands today as one of the all time great classics that has helped people through the generations to find prosperity</u>. Our golden classic (50th Reprint) contains original material not found in other reprints. This edition uses bold print all throughout the book to emphasize the Authors point.

Turning Fear into Power
""Turning Fear into power", was written by Richard lynch in 1932
<u>It provides straight forward strategies to overcome fear in all facets of life. This reprint is a one of a kind edition. It has been enhanced by writings added along the margins to strengthen the relevant points made by Lynch</u>. Grace M. Bosworth would strengthen each important point made by Lynch, sometimes just quoted words of wisdom, passages from the bible, or excerpts from other well known works. She was indeed a learned person and she knew what and where to insert her words to bring home the point being made in the book. This never before seen edition is now available for today's generation who are seeking freedom from fear.

Published Recovery Books

Off The Wall Contrarian quotes for people in Recovery
<u>The goal of this book is to provide the person working with an Alcohol Problem, more Tips, tactics and tools to strengthen recovery</u> (I am a recovering Alcoholic Sobriety date April 14th 1986)
This book is a collection of poignant, touching, and truthful thoughts and phrases related to the recovery process. Inspired by AA's 12-step program, this book provides hope and inspiration for anyone dealing with addiction and substance abuse issues. As with material presented in and around the rooms, it is suggested that you take what works and leave the rest. What does not work today may work for you tomorrow, which is why it is a good idea to pick up the book as often as you can. Program tools are a key to many people's recovery and this book gives you an opportunity to use several tools. 1) Reading recovery literature. 2) Writing- takes a quote each day, write it down

and carry it with you. 3) Meditation- by pondering or meditating on a quote you can improve your conscious contact with God. 4) Telephone- sharing a quote with a friend helps both. 5) Anonymity- many of the quotes and healing writings are from unknown authors. May their anonymity help you in your time of need.

The Food Contrarian
A book filled with tips, tactics and tools to help people with eating issues. It utilizes the 12 steps as a foundation and brings fresh ideas and strategies to assist the compulsive eater or non eater- (I lost two brothers form food related illnesses. I am also a grateful recovering compulsive overeater. In The program since March of 1991)
This book is a collection of poignant, touching, and truthful thoughts and phrases related to recovery from eating disorders or other food addictions. Inspired by AA's 12-step program, this book provides hope and inspiration for anyone dealing with food-related issues. 1) A dishonest mistake-- a lie. 2) Some people do the steps by sidestepping. 3) Count your blessings instead of counting your calories. 4) DIET: Doing Insane Eating Temporarily. 5) For the anorexic too little is too much. NOT FOR STUDY PURPOSES LIGHT READING WITH SERIOUS PONDERING Suggestion: Read one or two per day, write them down on a piece of paper and post or carry with you. 1) Relapse: When your disease is in recovery. 2) Binge: When enough is not enough. 3) Purge: An attempt to correct a mistake with another mistake. 4) Bulimia: Two wrongs to make right.

Relationship Recovery
This book is all encompassing and is suggested for anyone working a 12 step program of any kind as it is most likely that the problem has its roots in relationship to a greater or lesser degree. RELATIONSHIP RECOVERY is about using the 12-step program principles to help anyone suffering from relationship ills. While not approved by any 12-step program, it is a great addition to the literature offered to help in doing the steps, especially steps 3 through 12. Resolving relationship issues is the foundational key to any 12-step program, and recovery cannot occur without addressing it. This workbook is intended to help people in that endeavor.

Why Not Try God
The story of a man who found himself addicted to drug and alcohol and how he found recovery in the 12 step program. How he used program principles in all his affairs. Kreige suffered from mental disorders and used the principle of vigorous honesty that enabled him to lead a normal life. In addition the book has articles from Sam Shoemaker, Emmet Fox, Sybil Partridge and James Allen

Inspirational/Motivational books

Tuchy's Law
Tuchy's Law is a collection of quotes that spoke to me over a 40 year period from 1960 to 2000. The quotes covered all aspects of life and were from my point of view wise words. The quotes are from a few famous people, but mostly the people in my life that crossed my path. It is a life-affirming and thought-provoking collection of quips, quotes, and proverbs that were gathered and honed by me and my family, friends, and colleagues over a 25-year period. Covering topics as

diverse as ambition, success, initiative, and handling setbacks, the more than one thousand warm and witty sayings in this book will bring a smile to your face and leave you nodding in recognition.

The platinum Rule and other Contrarian Quotes

This is a collection of contrarian quotes many Fields contrarian quote was "If at first you do not succeed, try again, then give up and don't make a fool of yourself.

Another is The Platinum rule "do unto others as they would have you do unto them" these were gathered over the same 40 year period It is a warm, witty, and life-affirming collection of quips, quotes, and aphorisms that will touch your heart and bring a smile to your face. Gathered and honed by the Author over a 40-year period, the 522 sayings in this book will bring back fond memories on the topics of family, work, self-worth, dealing with adversity, aging gracefully, and many, many more.

Josephine in Her Words.

Josephine in Her words is a collection of words of Wisdom and related comments that Mom had given us over the last 60 years. It was a 90th birthday gift to Mom. The reviews on mom's book started what I refer to as interactive books/workbook

I essence it was a method of enabling the reader record any thoughts desires and memories that came about while reading the quotes and words of wisdom.

Phil in His Words Our Dad

An interactive book that enables the reader to write down words of wisdom from his /her dads that were triggered as the wisdom words of my Dad was read. Writing is an excellent way to bring back a deceased parent. Dad had been gone 15 years when this book was created. The source of the book was from several people who knew dad. As an experiment we took The Grandchildren and the Great Grandchildren that were too young to remember dad, and read highlights of the book to them. The result was phenomenal. Dad was transformed from being just a picture on the wall to a real person who had passed down ways of being to there Moms/Dads and grandparents

The words and wisdom of a devoted father collected and recorded by a loving son, PHIL, IN HIS WORDS: OUR DAD will resonate with adult children of all ages and backgrounds who remember and appreciate the gifts given to them by their parents. So often it is the wisdom of our fathers, grandfathers, mothers, and grandmothers that encouraged us to take the right path in life. The reading of Phil's words may trigger the words that were given to you, the reader. You are encouraged to write them down to reflect on, to pass on to your children, and to share with friends. You are encouraged to write down your favorite words to pass on to future generations. Enjoy Phil's words and may they help you in some way.

Sex and Intimacy

A serious and yet light hearted book of tactics, techniques and tools to make relationships work better. It approaches sex and Intimacy with great words of wisdom from people in all walks of life. Many words brought humor and lightness to this hard and hot topic

The words in Sex and Intimacy: The Gifts of Life are given by wise men, famous people, and common folks and are intended to give the reader truisms, advice, and comfort in the areas of sex and intimacy. It is our belief that sex and intimacy are God-given gifts to be enjoyed as any other gift. We also believe that the healthier people's sex lives are, the happier and healthier people are in all aspects of life. Recent research verifies the benefits of having sex on a regular basis. Sex can be fun, exciting, and a great way to become closer with your partner. Sex can also be great for your health, since your sexual health and mental well-being are closely linked. You are encouraged to use this interactive book to jot down and record ideas which, when implemented, would make your sex life healthier and happier.

Money and So much more- The real meaning of wealth

A book filled with wisdom from the famous and not so famous from ancient times and from current times. Again the goal of the book is to inspire people to put money in its right place, not have it rule them and how to be wise with money

Through these words the reader is moved to be different in the world and that money will take its appropriate place in life, thus allowing one to be free of money's grip.

Oprah in Her Words- our American Princess

Many of Oprah's wise words are enhanced by the Addition of Suggested affirmations, inquiries, and suggested action. The Goal of the book is to Make Oprah's words personal to the reader by giving suggestions and allowing interactivity through writing in the book in the appropriate space.
Readers are given space in which to create or to take on their own affirmations, inquiries, and actions. The book is divided into challenging topics with words designed to inspire, encourage, and assist.

Obama in His Words- pre -Election

Filled with the quotes, speeches and words that he used that helped him win the election. The Goal of the book was to go beyond the pictures and create a historical keepsake of his words

Satisfying Success

This book helps the reader to find the rare space of creating success that satisfies rather than success that is empty

Success is one of the strangest phenomenons in life. First, it is often subjective, and it has been elusive for many as it is often not well defined. Many who work their whole lives finally achieve it, only to find that it is a hollow victory, void of any satisfaction. In this inspiring and thought-provoking book one can discover the paths to satisfying success. You are encouraged to take from the words of others those that resonate for you and leave the ones that do not. You can indeed have both success and satisfaction at the same time. This book proves that it can be done and has been done for others.

Quotes to Live, Love, and Laugh By

Quotes to live love and laugh by are a collection of quotes regarded by many as the most impactful. The purpose of this collection is to lay out words to make a difference in many aspects of the reader's life. May one or more of these words make a difference in your life. The opportunity to make a difference in one's life is the source of my greatest pleasure.

Made in the USA
Lexington, KY
02 September 2014